The Life of a 1966 Corvette

Paul M. Fritz

Copyright © 2017 Paul M. Fritz.

All rights reserved. No part of this book may be reproduced, stored, or transmitted by any means—whether auditory, graphic, mechanical, or electronic—without written permission of the author, except in the case of brief excerpts used in critical articles and reviews. Unauthorized reproduction of any part of this work is illegal and is punishable by law.

ISBN: 978-0-5781-8759-4 (sc)
ISBN: 978-0-5781-8758-7 (e)

Library of Congress Control Number: 2017904353

Paul M. Fritz
20622 Davidway
Lexington Park, Maryland 20653-2635

Ordering Information:
Special discounts are available on quantity purchases by corporations, associations, educators, and others.
For details, contact the publisher at the above listed address.
US trade bookstores and wholesalers:
Please contact Paul M. Fritz Tel: (301) 737-0444;
Fax: (301) 737-7802 or e-mail thefritzkid@gmail.com

Because of the dynamic nature of the Internet, any web addresses or links contained in this book may have changed since publication and may no longer be valid. The views expressed in this work are solely those of the author and do not necessarily reflect the views of the publisher, and the publisher hereby disclaims any responsibility for them.

Any people depicted in stock imagery provided by Thinkstock are models, and such images are being used for illustrative purposes only.
Certain stock imagery © Thinkstock.

Rev. date: 5/01/2017

2013 NCRS National Meet, Hampton, VA
Ron Dill. Used with permission.

In memory of Mom and Dad,
Georgianna L. and Paul R. Fritz,
and
in memory of many discussions with Mom and Dad, the pastor,
and me about the pros and cons of purchasing the Corvette.
For them allowing me to make the final decision to purchase the Corvette.

Georgianna L.

Paul R.

CONTENTS

Acknowledgments vi
Introduction vii

Chapter 1	Specification Guide	1
Chapter 2	History of Ownership	6
Chapter 3	Restoration Story	14
Chapter 4	Maintenance	31
Chapter 5	National Corvette Restorers Society (NCRS)	33
Chapter 6	National Corvette Restorers Society (NCRS) Awards and Events	69
Chapter 7	Photo Shoot, *Rolling Stone*/Chevrolet 2004 Calendar—The Year In Rock	89
Chapter 8	Photo Shoot, the Danbury Mint Corvette Models	103
Chapter 9	Other Awards	109
Chapter 10	Special Memories over the Years	110
Appendix A	Websites with My 1966 Corvette	118
Appendix B	New Addition to Paul's Garage	119
Appendix C	Cool Corvette Adventures in the Fast Lane	122
Appendix D	Photographers	127

References 128

List of Figures

Figure 1. Specifications Guide, 1966 Corvette Stingray Coupe VIN 194376S115422 2
Figure 2. 1966 Specification Guide 3
Figure 3. History of ownership 7
Figure 4. Titles and bills of sales 8

ACKNOWLEDGMENTS

Many talented and generous artisans contributed their expertise to the success of this restoration and process of obtaining the National Corvette Restorers Society (NCRS), Zora Arkus-Duntov Mark of Excellence Award (restored 1953–1974) for my Corvette.

I'm particularly indebted to Zach for his generous support, encouragement, and expertise in repairing and maintaining the high-quality condition of the Corvettes. I am truly grateful for a friend and buddy like you.

Thank you to Dave at The Vette Shop for his attention to detail and untiring effort to complete a NCRS quality restoration.

Thank you to Sean, The Vette Shop owner, for allowing me to work in the shop during the restoration.

Tom, thank you for the opportunity to share my knowledge of the NCRS judging process during the preparation of your 1995 Corvette, for the experiences on the road trips to NCRS meetings to obtain your award, and especially for the experiences of changing flat tires along the highway.

I am thankful to many others in the Corvette community and my family.

Last but not least, a special thank you for my friend and travel partner during the long road trips, Debra, who took many of the great photographs that document the many hard miles traveled to obtain this NCRS award. Thank you for putting up with me when things didn't go right.

INTRODUCTION

I have owned this 1966 Sunfire Yellow 427 cubic inch, 425 horsepower Corvette Coupe for over forty-seven years. During that time, I served twenty-one years in the United States Navy as a Senior Chief Petty Officer, Aviation Electronics Technician, with experience and attention to detail as an electronics technician, air crewman, technical writer, and maintenance technician. I was responsible for troubleshooting and repairing all types of aircraft failures, as well as writing and teaching maintenance procedures for both military and civilian aircraft.

I have spent many years maintaining my own trucks and cars. My attention to detail is demonstrated in the care and maintenance of this beautiful '66 Corvette. In addition to receiving the NCRS Zora Arkus-Duntov Mark of Excellence Award in 2005, I was invited by Chevrolet to provide the '66 for 2003 photo shoots by the Danbury Mint models and for the cover of the 2004 *Rolling Stone*/Chevrolet "Year in Rock" calendar. At several "fun shows," 2000 – 2016 I received Best of Show trophies and first place in class trophies. I was also invited to the Delaware Valley Chapter NCRS, 2002 Gallery II and 2016 Gallery XVI as an example of a Corvette that achieved the NCRS Zora Arkus-Duntov Mark of Excellence Award in Carlisle, Pennsylvania.

The Life of a 1966 Corvette includes previous owners, purchase information, the restoration project, NCRS judging guidelines, photo shoots, and the path to the NCRS Zora Arkus-Duntov Mark of Excellence Award, including the special people who helped make it happen.

My love affair with the Corvette started back in 1963. A local owner of a 1963 Saddle Tan, 327 cubic inch engine with fuel-injected coupe would park his Corvette next to the bank in Schuylkill Haven, Pennsylvania, on Friday nights for all to gaze at. My friends and I would gather around, careful not to get too close, and just stare for what seemed like hours, drooling over the beautiful lines and bragging about owning one like it someday. I remember telling my friends many times that I would own a Corvette like that one someday. Their response was always the same: "Keep on dreaming. You cannot afford the price."

As I grew older, the dream to have a Corvette grew much stronger. I was still in high school when the next generation C 3 styling for Corvette's third generation would be based on the Mako Shark II came out. I was disappointed with the pointed nose and rear window. Just out of high school and with little or no money, what would be the chances of getting a C 2 Corvette with beautiful bubble hood and boat tail like rear end? A very slim to no chance!

The cost of a new Corvette was in excess of $5,000. Working full-time, I started to save money toward buying a car. However, it was difficult with a steady girlfriend who enjoyed doing things and going places.

On one of our nights out, we were discussing what kind of car we would like to have one day. Her choice was a Karmann Ghia that she thought her father would have gotten her for graduation. Of course my dream car was one like that 1963 Corvette. Working at a manufacturing plant assembly line, assembling heating units, money was good for the times. Most went to savings. Then in January 1969, I purchased a 1957 Chevy coupe with a 327 cubic inch engine with a four-speed transmission. It was a nice set of wheels but no Corvette.

Sometime in July 1969, on the way to work I passed the used car lot of Dinger Chevrolet Inc. in Schuylkill Haven, Pennsylvania, and there was a C 2 Corvette coupe for sale. Not any Corvette but a 1966 Corvette Stingray, 427 cubic inch, 425 horsepower, Sunfire Yellow Coupe. My dream Corvette was a 327 cubic inch, red coupe with standard exhaust. The Corvette on the lot was a coupe with a big block, 427 cubic inch, side exhaust pipes, black interior, beautiful bubble hood and Sunfire Yellow color. I decided to stop and see how much they were asking for this beauty. While I was drooling over the Corvette, a salesman came out, and we discussed the options and beauty. Finally I asked what the price was. To my surprise, the asking price was only $3295. The wheels started turning in my head. I had a little over $3,000 in the bank. *Wonder if Mom and Dad would let me use that money to buy the Corvette.* That night I talked to Mom and Dad about the Corvette on the used car lot. I asked Dad if he would check it out. His answer was, "What are you going to do with that kind of car?"

He did not say one way or the other if he would stop and look at it or not. After work that night, I talked with Dad. We discussed the pros and cons of getting the Corvette and the cost. Unbeknownst to me, he had stopped and inquired about the Corvette and was given the price of $2995. Things were looking better. *Maybe there is a chance to get a Corvette similar to my dream Corvette.* After much discussion, both Mom and Dad agreed to let me withdraw the money from my saving account (see chapter 2, figure 4). Dad took me down to the used car lot to buy the Corvette. It was still there, looking beautiful.

When we told the salesman we wanted to purchase the Corvette, he said the price was $3295 and he would write it up. Good thing Dad was with me. Dad asked about the increase from what he was quoted the other day. The answer from the salesman was, "We did not realize what we had." Dad said, "Sorry, you gave me the price of $2995, and that's what we will pay for the Corvette." That's the reason for the bill of sale being in Dad's name and the title in mine. The date was July 29, 1969 (see chapter 2, figures 3 and 4).

The summer passed, and I had my dream car—a 1966 Sunfire Yellow Coupe 427 cubic inch, side exhaust pipes and all. October came with rumors that my draft notice would be in the mail in November 1969. I was going to be drafted in accordance with one of Dad's friends on the draft board. I went off to the recruiting offices to see if I could get a good deal on education in the aviation field if I enlisted. The navy offered the best opportunity to get the aviation mechanic school after boot camp if I agreed to enlist now. So I enlisted in the United States Navy on October 23, 1969, and the Corvette went into storage.

Several times over the next four years, when I was on leave, she came out of storage. In November 1974, the Corvette was placed in a more permanent storage, as my navy career was taking me overseas for a period of time. The Corvette stayed in storage for the next thirty-plus years as I spent twenty-one years and eight days in the navy. Who's counting? After retiring from the navy, adjusting to civilian life was a challenge, and again money was an issue due to some difficult times.

Then on November 13, 1998, the '66 Corvette came out of storage, and the full body off the frame restoration began at The Vette Shop in Warminster, Pennsylvania. During the restoration, we decided to follow the process of the NCRS judging (refer to chapter 5, "NCRS Judging Information").

And now the photos and documentation tell the rest of the story.

Stone Mountain, Georgia
Copyright © 2003. Photograph by Debra Wood. Using with permission.

2003 Stone Mountain, Georgia
Copyright © 2003. Photograph by Debra Wood. Using with permission.

Specification Guide

During the restoration, we did not find a build sheet under the fuel tank. However, it was possible to develop a list or build sheet during the restoration by recording the part numbers, RPO numbers, descriptions, casting numbers, and manufacture dates because this Corvette was unmolested and estimated to be all original. From the collection of this information, we were able to develop a specification guide or build sheet for this vehicle identification number (VIN), a 1966 Corvette Coupe.

Figure 1.
Specifications Guide, 1966 Corvette Stingray Coupe VIN 194376S115422

RPO #	Description	Quantity	Cost
984	Sunfire Yellow	2,339	
	Interior STD Black Vinyl		
19437	Base Corvette Coupe	9,958	$4265.00
	Destination Charge to Yukon, OK		57.75
A01	Soft Ray Tinted Glass, all windows	11,859	15.80
F41	Special Front and Rear Suspension	2,705	36.90
G81	Positraction Rear Axle	24,056	42.15
K66	Transistor Ignition System	7,146	73.75
L72	427 cubic inch 425 horsepower	5,258	312.85
M21	4 Speed Manual Transmission	10,837	184.35
N14	Side Mount Exhaust System	3,617	131.65
P92	Whitewall Tires, 7.75x15 (rayon cord)	17,969	31.30
U69	AM/FM Radio	26,363	199.10
	Wheels, Steel: 15x51/2 "JK" with Hubcaps		
	Total Cost		$5350.60

Build date: G01 - 02 March 1966 St Louis, MO

Fritz Purchase Date: 29 July 1969

Figure 2
1966 Specification Guide

RPO #	Options/Equipment	Quantity	Cost
900	Tuxedo Black	1,190	
972	Ermine White	2,120	
974	Rally Red	3,366	
976	Nassau Blue	6,100	
978	Laguna Blue	2,054	
980	Throphy Blue	1,463	
982	Mosport Green	2,311	
984	Sunfire Yellow	2,339	
986	Silver Pearl	2,937	
988	Milano Maroon	3,799	
	Unknown Special Paint or Primer	11	
19437	Coupe	9,958	$4,265.00
19567	Convertible	17,762	$4,084.00
Base	300 HP 327 cu.in. engine	9,755	No charge
Base	Three Speed Transmission	564	No charge
Base	Black Folding Top*	7,259	No charge
Base	Vinyl Trim	25,718	No charge
---	Leather Seat Trim	2,002	$79.00
A01	Soft Ray Tinted Glass	11,859	$15.80
A02	Soft Ray Tinted Windshield	9.270	$10.55
A31	Power Windows	4,562	$57.95
A82	Headrests	1,003	$42.15
A85	Shoulder Harness	37	$26.35
C05	Colored Folding Top*	9,200	No charge
C05	White (In place of Black)	8,789	No charge
C05	Beige Folding Top (In place of Black)	411	No charge
C07	Auxiliary Hardtop*	8,453	
C07	In place of Soft Top	1,303	No charge
	In addition to Soft Top	7,160	$231.75

Figure 2
1966 Specification Guide

RPO #	Options/Equipment	Quantity	Cost
C48	Heater Delete (credit)	54	$97.85
C60	Air Conditioning	3,520	$412.90
	With Coupes	2138	
	With Convertibles	1,382	
F41	Special Suspension	2,705	$36.90
G81	Positraction Rear Axle	24,056	$42.15
	With 3.08:1 Ratio	2,385	
	With 3.36:1 Ratio	8,538	
	With 3.55:1 Ratio	3,119	
	With 3.70:1 Ratio	6,612	
	With 4.11:1 Ratio	3,310	
	With 4.56:1 Ratio	91	
J50	Power Brakes	5,464	$42.15
J56	Heavy-Duty Brakes	382	$342.30
K19	Air Injector Reactor	2,380	$44.75
K66	Transistor Ignition	7,146	$73.75
L36	390 Horsepower 427 Cubic-Inch Engine	5,116	$181.20
L72	425 Horsepower 427 cubic inch Engine	5,258	$312.85
L79	350 Horsepower 327 cu. In. Engine	7,591	$105.35
M20	Manual Transmission Wide-Ratio Four-Speed	10,837	$184.35
M21	Manual Transmission Close-Ratio Four-Speed	13,903	$184.35
M22	Manual Transmission Heavy-Duty Four-Speed	15	$237.00
M35	Power glide	2,401	$194.85
	With 300 Horsepower	2,381	
	With 390 Horsepower	20	
NO3	36 Gallon Fuel Tank**	66	$198.05
N11	Off Road Exhaust System	2,795	$36.90
N14	Side-Mounted Exhaust System	3,617	$131.65
N36	Teakwood Steering Wheel	3,941	$47.40

Figure 2
1966 Specification Guide

RPO #	Options/Equipment	Quantity	Cost
N36	Telescopic Steering Column	3,670	$42.15
N40	Power Steering	5,611	$94.80
P48	Aluminum Knock-Off Wheels (5)	1,194	$316.00
P92	7.75-15" Rayon Whitewall Tires	17,969	$31.30
T01	7.75-15" Gold stripe Tires	5,557	$46.55
U69	AM-FM Radio	26,363	$199.10
V74	Traffic Hazard Lamps	5,764	$11.60

(*) Convertible Only (**) Coupe Only

Price Effective Date
March 16, 1966

Copyright © NCRS. Used with permission.

CHAPTER 2

History of Ownership

Just like a family has a family tree, this Corvette has a history of owners, or a family tree, which I was able to develop. After the restoration was complete, The Vette Shop's owner, Sean Farrell, asked if they could take the Corvette to the Atlantic City Show and Auction in February 2000 as an example of the restoration work they perform. At the show, many people came up to me and asked if the Corvette was for sale and how much it was going for. The answer was always the same: "What part of 'not for sale' do you not understand?" One of the people inquiring was Mr. Stoudt from Stoudt Auto Sales, Inc., in Reading, Pennsylvania. He said he remembered the Corvette. It was one that he had sold many years earlier. He asked if it was for sale and got the same answer as the others. He commented that if I ever wanted to sell it, I should give him a call. We discussed the history of ownership for a short period. I had many questions for him. Then I asked if he might have any records from 1969 when he sold it. He gave me his business card and said to call him Monday with the vehicle identification number (VIN) and he would check his records. Monday I called Mr. Stoudt and asked him to check his file for any documentation on this Corvette. He said that it would take several days but he would get back to me. To my surprise, at the end of the week there was a letter in the mail with copies of the owner's registration and bills of sale enclosed for three sales in 1969. With this information and the NCRS shipping data report, I was able to develop a history or family tree of the Corvette. I am still missing ownership details from March 2, 1966, to January 2, 1969.

Think about the period of time during which this Corvette changed owners so often. They were when the military was serving in Vietnam. Returning home with large savings, they would purchase sports cars. Many had to trade in the sports cars for family cars.

I purchased this Corvette from a dealer when the previous owner, who was becoming a family man, traded it in for a 1969 Chevrolet Chevelle 396 Super Sport (SS).

Figure 3.
History of ownership

March 2, 1966: GM official production date (NCRS shipping data report dated November 18, 2010)

March 1966: Original delivery—dealer code 51, zone 23, R. T. Ayers Chevrolet, Yukon, Oklahoma

March 2, 1966–January 1, 1969: History unknown

January 2, 1969: Calhoun Motors, 470 Calhoun Street, Trenton, New Jersey

January 3, 1969: Stoudt Auto Sales, Inc., Warren and Carbon Streets, Reading, Pennsylvania

January 24, 1969: Harold Stump, Shillington, Pennsylvania

March 1969: Stoudt Auto Sales, Inc., Warren and Carbon Streets, Reading, Pennsylvania

March 18, 1969: Warren Kraft, Schuylkill Haven, Pennsylvania

July 1969: Dinger Chevrolet, Schuylkill Haven, Pennsylvania

July 29, 1969: Paul Robert Fritz, R. D. Number 1, Schuylkill Haven, Pennsylvania (Dad)

July 29, 1969: Bill of sale, Dinger Chevrolet to Paul Robert Fritz (Dad)

July 29, 1969: First National Bank, Schuylkill Haven, Pennsylvania, $3,000 withdrawal

July 29, 1969: Paul Martin Fritz, R. D. Number 1, Schuylkill Haven, Pennsylvania (Son) Pennsylvania title

Registration: Pennsylvania antique plate—31HL

July 14, 2001: Owner—Paul Fritz. Previous owners—Warren Kraft, Harold Stump, Skyline Drive Corvettes, Twenty-Second Annual Twilight In-Vette-Tational, Reading, Pennsylvania

Figure 4.
Titles and bills of sales

Calhoun Motors sales contract to Stoudt Auto Sales, Inc.

Bill of sale, Stoudt Auto Sales, Inc. to Harold Stump

Bill of sale, Stoudt Auto Sales, Inc. to Warren Kraft

Bill of sale, Dinger Chevrolet Inc. to Paul R. Fritz

Bankbook showing withdrawal for payment

Certificate of title, Paul M. Fritz

Window sticker (reproduction)

March 1966, the GM official production date
(NCRS shipping data report letter dated November 18, 2010)

January 2, 1969, bill of sale, Calhoun Motors,
470 Calhoun Street, Trenton, New Jersey

January 24, 1969, bill of sale,
Harold Stump, Shillington, Pennsylvania

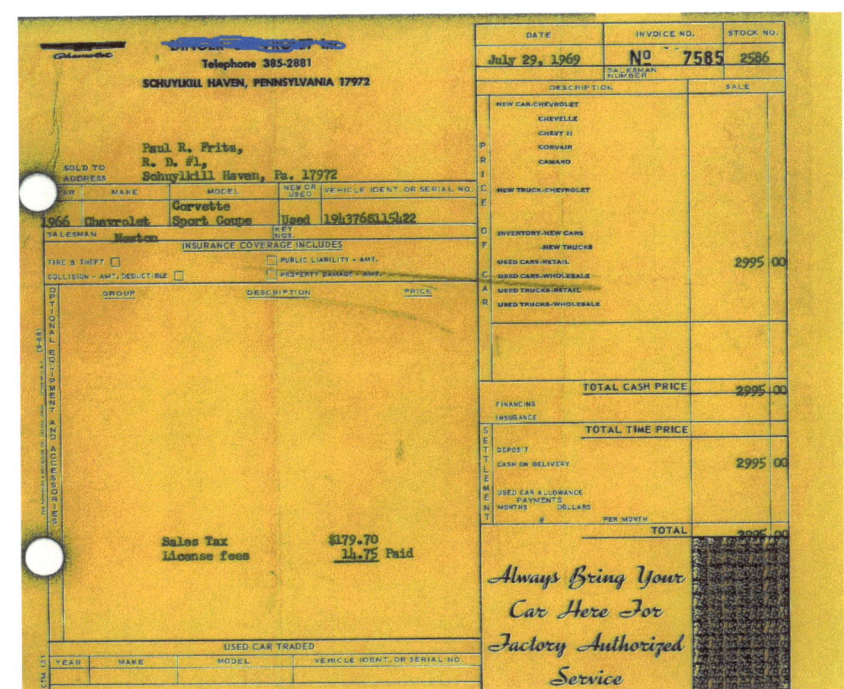

March 18, 1969, bill of sale, Warren Kraft, Schuylkill Haven, Pennsylvania

July 29, 1969, bill of sale, Dinger Chevrolet to Paul Robert Fritz (Dad)

July 29, 1969, $3,000 withdrawal from my account, First National Bank, Schuylkill Haven, Pennsylvania

July 29, 1969, Paul Martin Fritz, R. D. Number 1, Schuylkill Haven, Pennsylvania (son), Pennsylvania title

Registration, Pennsylvania antique plate, 31HL

July 14, 2001, owner—Paul Fritz. Previous owners—Warren Kraft, Harold Stump, Skyline Drive Corvettes, Twenty-Second Annual Twilight In-Vette-Tational, Reading, Pennsylvania. Copyright © 2001. Photograph by Eileen. Used with permission.

CHAPTER 3

Restoration Story

The restoration of the Corvette at The Vette Shop started on November 13, 1998, when it was taken out of storage. It had been placed in storage at the start of my service in the United States Navy on October 23, 1969, and remained in storage until November 13, 1998. Several times during this period, it was moved to different storage areas. After my retirement from the United States Navy, the Corvette remained in storage in a friend's barn. I was divorced in December 1994, but the Corvette survived the property settlement.

On November 13, 1998, I took the Corvette out of storage to start the restoration process at The Vette Shop in Warminster, Pennsylvania. On long weekends off, I would travel back to The Vette Shop from Patuxent River, Maryland, to work on the Corvette. Dave and Sean were very good to allow me to work in the garage with them. During the disassembly, we discovered it was an all-original '66 Corvette. This led us to restore it to the original specifications in accordance with the National Corvette Restorers Society (NCRS) judging manual and *GM Assembly Manual*.

Since we had decided the direction to go was back to original, finances became an issue. The Navy Federal Credit Union (NFCU) came to the rescue. They agreed the appraisal and the title would provide the basis for a loan of half the appraised value with a payback of five years. This would allow for the completion of the restoration and not cause a financial burden.

The restoration was completed on March 3, 2000. I did not have an enclosed trailer to haul my Corvette back to Patuxent River, Maryland. A friend used his truck and trailer to pick up my Corvette at The Vette Shop and return to Maryland. Shortly after getting the Corvette back, I purchased an eight-by-twenty-four Cargo Mate trailer, often referred to as the big white box because of its size. After several trips to NCRS meetings, the big white box had to go. I purchased a black, low-profile, V-nose, all-aluminum eight-by-eighteen Trailex. What a difference in towing—a real pleasure.

The following photos tell the restoration story and show the attention to detail.

On Friday, November 13, 1998, the Corvette came out of storage and was taken to The Vette Shop in Warminster, Pennsylvania, for restoration.

When The Vette Shop got the Corvette, it was completely intact except for aluminum, slotted wheels, and yellow metal-flake paint being changed from original.

The disassembly of the Corvette began.
Copyright © 1998. Photograph by The Vette Shop. Used with permission.

Internal gauge cluster, clock, radio console, and glove box were removed.
All components will be restored to new condition.
Copyright © 1998. Photograph by The Vette Shop. Used with permission.

The interior was completely gutted. Driver's compartment is on the left side; passenger's side is on the right. Notice the piece of fiberglass quarter panel on the floor of the driver's side. I will show its purpose later in this story. Note the trim tabs remain in place on passenger's side glove-box support.
Copyright © 1998. Photograph by The Vette Shop. Used with permission.

The coupe body is being separated from the chassis. The stripping of the metal-flake paint has begun.
Copyright © 1998. Photograph by The Vette Shop. Used with permission.

Original, complete 1966 chassis and 427 cubic inch, 425 horsepower engine before disassembly.
Notice the corrosion and dirt after approximately thirty years in storage.
Copyright © 1998. Photograph by The Vette Shop. Used with permission.

Original, complete 1966 chassis and 427 cubic inch, 425 horsepower engine before Disassembly.
Copyright © 1998. Photograph by The Vette Shop. Used with permission.

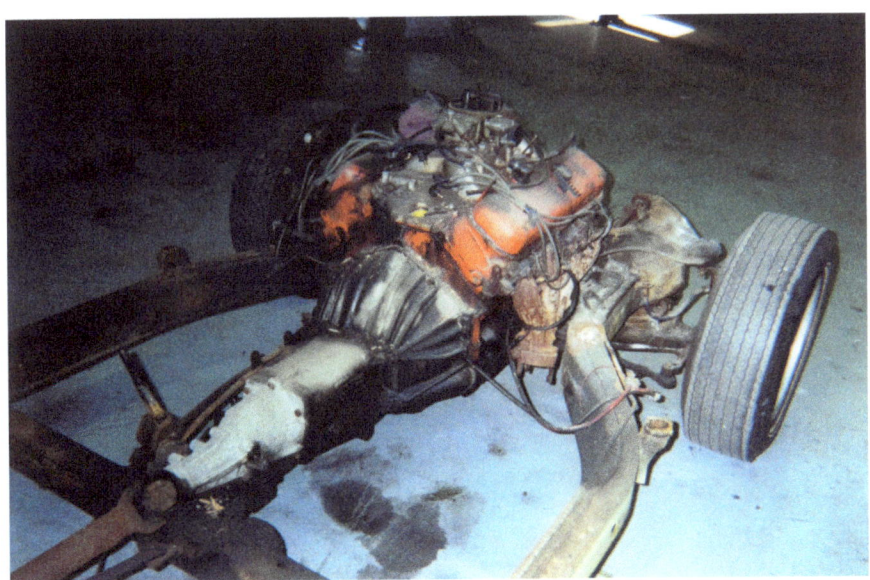

Original, complete 1966 chassis and 427 cubic inch, 425 horsepower engine before disassembly
Copyright © 1998. Photograph by The Vette Shop. Used with permission.

Original, complete 1966 chassis, rear-end housing and fuel tank.
Copyright © 1998. Photograph by The Vette Shop. Used with permission.

Original 1966 bare chassis before restoration.
Copyright © 1998. Photograph by The Vette Shop. Used with permission.

Original 1966 bare chassis after sandblasting.
Copyright © 1998. Photograph by The Vette Shop. Used with permission.

Original 1966 chassis after painting.
Copyright © 1998. Photograph by The Vette Shop. Used with permission.

The coupe's body has been removed from the chassis and installed on a body chassis. Original paint has been hand-stripped down to the original baked-on red primer. The body is checked for cracks or damage and repaired.
Copyright © 1998. Photograph by The Vette Shop. Used with permission.

The left front bumper bolt hole required repair.
Copyright © 1998. Photograph by The Vette Shop. Used with permission.

The hole was enlarged and had some soft fiberglass.
Remember the piece of fiberglass quarter panel in the driver's compartment?
Copyright © 1998. Photograph by The Vette Shop. Used with permission.

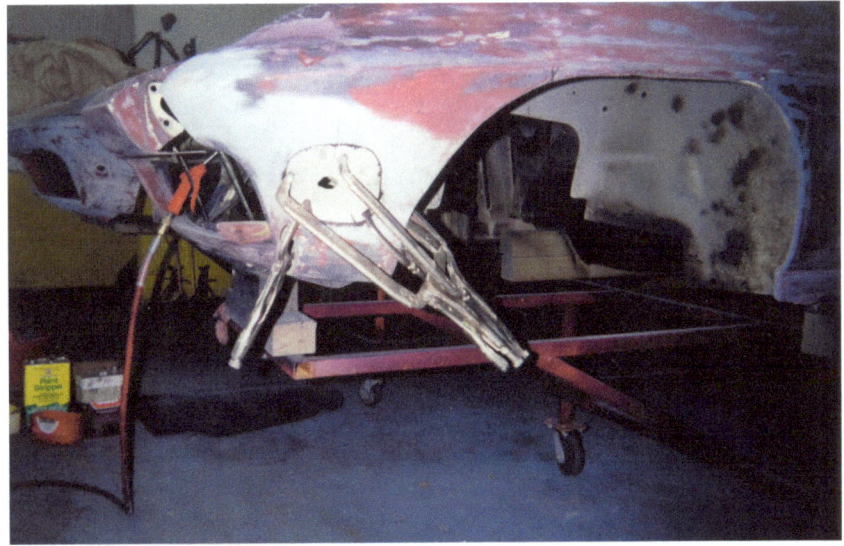

It was used as a donor to keep all the fiberglass original. Nice fit. Good job.
Copyright © 1998. Photograph by The Vette Shop. Used with permission.

Body repairs complete, ready for final sanding and red oxide primer.
Copyright © 1999. Photograph by The Vette Shop. Used with permission.

The red oxide primer was thoroughly sanded in preparation for the Sunfire lacquer paint job.
Copyright © 1999. Photograph by The Vette Shop. Used with permission.

Now all the jams have been sprayed in with Sunfire Yellow paint.
Copyright © 1999. Photograph by The Vette Shop. Used with permission.

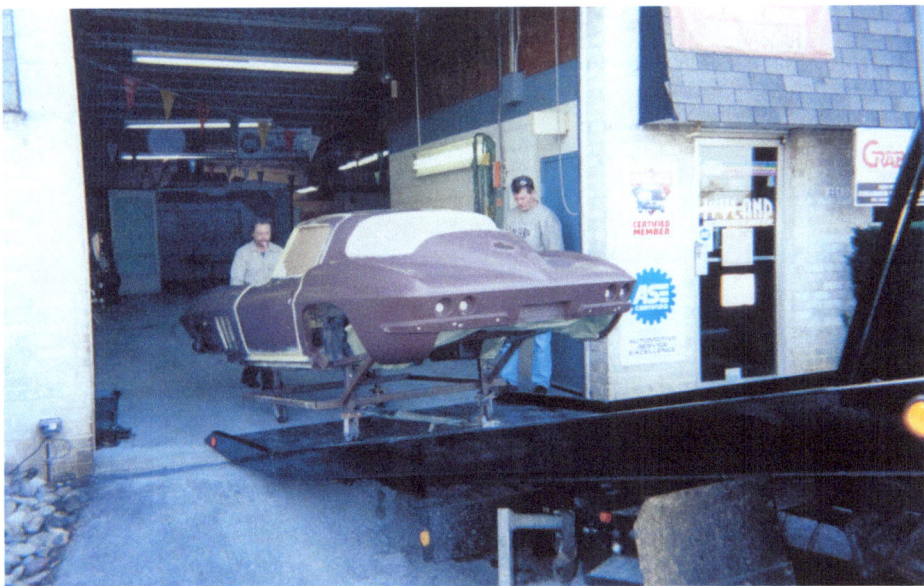
Dave and Sean loading the body onto a rollback truck for the trip to the paint booth.

Sean and Dave with the Corvette in the paint booth. "Now what are we going to do?"

"Dave, can you smell the fresh lacquer paint?" The Corvette body in the paint booth after a long day of painting.

Several days later, Dave and Sean offloading the body on return trip from the paint booth.
Copyright © 1999. Photograph by The Vette Shop. Used with permission.

Paul and Dave installing side exhaust pipes.
Copyright © 1999. Photograph by The Vette Shop. Used with permission.

Paul adding oil to the rebuilt 427 cubic inch engine.
Copyright © 1999. Photograph by The Vette Shop. Used with permission.

Chassis after restoration.

Dave and Paul with The Vette Shop display of the completed restored rolling chassis to the Cavalcade of Corvettes, Delaware Valley Corvette Show at Willow Grove, Pennsylvania.
Copyright © 1999. Photograph by The Vette Shop. Used with permission.

At last the body and chassis are coming back together.
Copyright © 1999. Photograph by The Vette Shop. Used with permission.

Body and chassis back together.

The finished Sunfire Yellow Corvette on display at the 2000 Atlantic City Show and Auction, February 2000.

CHAPTER 4

Maintenance

Maintenance Issues

You might think that after a complete body-off restoration, maintenance should be at a minimum. Don't be fooled. We are dealing with a piece of machinery, a Corvette, that is fifty-plus years old. All the original parts were completely disassembled and rebuilt to original specifications and cleaned, painted, and plated as required. You would think that after all the work that went into the restoration, that maintenance would be minor. Wrong answer. Beyond the normal maintenance like cleaning, polishing, vacuum the interior, wiping down the engine and engine bay, waxing, wiping down the chassis, checking the oil, and checking the air pressure in the tires, other issues came up.

Going through the NCRS judging routine working toward the Zora Arkus-Duntov Mark of Excellence Award, there were minor details to repair and/or replace. We experienced things like windshield wipers out of alignment when in the parked position, parking brake not holding properly, Holly carburetor leaking, and the fan clutch leaking and out of alignment.

Some major issues came up when attempting to pass the performance verification (PV).

We were unable to take the engine over the 5,000 rpm in first gear as required to pass the ten-mile portion of the PV. We found several cracks on the aluminum intake manifold, tore down the engine, took the manifold to get repaired, and reassembled the engine. This was done at least three time before we found the cause: overheating.

We needed to troubleshoot the water leak under the bell housing. We removed the transmission and bell housing to gain access to the upper-right freeze plug. We found a sand-like material in the engine block, which in turn clogged the cooling ports in the heads. This explained the overheating and the cracked intake manifold. We pulled the engine block and did a complete rebuild, the way it should have been done in the first place. Sometimes it has to be done my way or else.

There were leaking brake calibers due to the long delay in getting the engine rebuilt. We removed and replaced brake calibers with new original parts.

The fan clutch was leaking. We removed it, sent it out for rebuilding, and reinstalled it.

The main rear oil seal was leaking due to an incorrect oil pan. We removed the incorrect oil pan and replaced the main oil seal. We repaired the original oil pan and reinstalled it.

Sloppy steering found deteriorating steering coupler (rag joint) and leaking steering box. We removed the steering box and sent out to be rebuilt. We reinstalled the steering box. We removed and replaced the rag joint.

There were fuel leaks. The first leak was the sending unit in the tank that had a cold solider joint on the feed tube. We removed, repaired, and reinstalled. The second fuel issue was a corroded fuel tank. We removed it and replaced it with a new fuel tank.

Parts

Keeping the Corvette to NCRS judging requirements means looking all over for replacement parts that are sometimes difficult to find. Thank goodness for fellow Corvette owners that have extra parts in their garages and are willing to help you with your repairs. Also, there are several parts suppliers available.

It is not like your new car or truck that you can take to the dealer for repairs. All the dealer has to do is call the warehouse or local part store and remove and replace the failed parts, and you are on your way.

Zach's Garage has been the source for all the maintenance and repairs. It is very rewarding to have friends like Zach and his knowledge of Corvettes. We have been helping each other out on many projects. During the rebuild of the engine, we put an extension on Zach's Garage where I was able to do all the insulation and help with the sheet rocking.

Thanks, buddy!

CHAPTER 5

National Corvette Restorers Society (NCRS)

Judging Information

Vital reference information for purchasing, restoring and authenticating your Corvette. Minute details uncovered during four decades of NCRS research into factory originality. Great Cars and Great Friends.

What to expect at a judging event:

Be patient. You will have five teams of two judges each, with the possibility of additional observer judge(s) on each team. Each team will cover one section of your score sheets; Operations, Interior, Exterior, Mechanical and Chassis. It may seem like an eternity between judging teams, however, be assured the team leader is trying to keep them moving at a steady pace.

The NCRS judges are under tremendous pressure. They must spend enough time with the car to be thorough and yet be quick and efficient. So, if the judge does not stay and chat, you will know why. Judges will briefly review your score sheet and explain each deduction they have taken upon completion of their section in judging. They will not be expected to spend an excess amount of time discussing the results, and for understandable reasons, will discuss these deductions with only the owner. You must initial your score sheets in order for them to be tabulated. Initialing the score sheet does not mean the owner agrees with the deductions, it only indicates the sheets have been presented to the owner by the judges and reviewed by the owner.

Dust can be experienced since judging is not held in a dust free environment. Light cleaning is permitted on the judging day. Mechanical repairs, assembling of cars, or replacing parts is not allowed.

Crowds can be large. There are typically a lot of people on the judging field, so plan for many people to be near your car.

Allow yourself enough time. Rushing and last minute details add to stress. Plan to be early and do not finish your restoration on the field. The more organized and prepared you are, the easier and more enjoyable things will be.

Remain with your car during judging, and if you must leave for any reason, be sure you inform the team leader.

Arrival

Check in at the event registration desk and also at the judging registration desk. Be sure to bring proof of ownership and current liability insurance. Read all information in the packets you receive pertaining to the event you are attending. Typically, you will receive an event and judging schedule at the time of registration.

Trailer parking will be controlled at each individual meet by the host chapter(s). Please abide by their request as congestion and confusion usually results when someone decides they do not have to abide by the rules.

Clean up facilities

A clean up area with water will be provided when logistically possible. You are allowed to do light cleaning all day during the judging process if you want. Less than 2% of your raw score is related to cleanliness. Therefore, cleanliness will not, by itself, keep you from earning any NCRS Award. Judges expect your car to be "dealer preparation for delivery clean", no more.

Advance preparation:

NCRS publishes two manuals that pertain to the judging of your car, both of which you need to read and understand. The first is the "Judging Reference Manual" which gives a thorough description of the judging process. The second manual is the "Corvette Technical Information Manual & Judging Guide" for the year of your car which describes the originality of each judged area on your car. These manuals and score sheets are available from the NCRS Online Store or the Membership Office. Use the sheets to judge your car. Be honest and critical. This pre-judging will give you a chance to fix last minute details before you come to the meet.

Controversial Items:

If you suspect something to be controversial about your Corvette, but you believe it to be historically authentic, please bring documentation to support your case. The burden of proof remains with the owner. The judges will decide whether or not to accept your proof, and there are numerous cases where it has been accepted.

About your judges:

Your judges will be the best available at the meet you are attending. Because this is an educational process when possible, we will team a Master Judge with a judge of less skill and, as mentioned earlier, there may also be observer judge(s). Remember you and the judges all belong to the same organization and you are all there because you choose to be. You will also meet the National Team Leader or his designated representative. This individual has the best understanding of our system and is your ear to bend in cases of judging disagreement. Once each team has completed their section, we need you to do something for us; "judge the judges". You will be supplied with a form on which you can rate your satisfaction with your judges. Please take this seriously. We cannot improve our system without honest input from you. When complete, give this form to your Team Leader.

Removal of parts:

In order to verify some numbers and component authenticity, you will be asked by the judge to remove such things as the air cleaner, spare tire, ignition shielding, etc. Rest assured, no significant disassembly will be required.

Stampings:

Please make sure your engine pad is free of all grease and dirt before arriving for judging. 1953 through 1976 must also be free of all paint. However, be cautious. Do not use tools or chemicals that could damage the pad finish. A painted, or otherwise obscured engine pad is an automatic 38 point deduction.

It may be necessary to lift a tracing of your engine pad. This is done by rubbing a pencil over Scotch tape placed on the pad. This causes no harm to the engine pad and will allow the judges to examine a clear impression of the pad.

Definitions of Counterfeit vs. Restoration:

NCRS does not consider the restoration or replacement of components as counterfeit as long as the intent is to restore the car to its former or original state as it left the factory.

To make this perfectly clear, read the following definitions from Webster's Dictionary and the accompanying examples.

Restore:

"To renew; to put back into existence or bring back to a former or original state".

For instance, the following examples represent restorations and are not considered counterfeiting:

Repainting an original black Corvette with black lacquer paint.

Installing accurately reproduced black vinyl seat covers in a car that left the factory with a standard black interior.

Counterfeit:

"To make an imitation of something else with the intent to deceive or defraud".

For instance, the following would be examples of counterfeiting:

Repainting an original blue car red and changing the trim tag to make red appear to be the original color.

Installing a red interior in a car that left the factory with a blue interior and changing the trim tag to make red appear to be the original color interior.

Replacing the engine of an original small block Corvette with a big block and stamping numbers on it to make it appear to be an original big block engine.

Replacing the carburetor on an engine with a fuel injection unit and stamping the numbers and suffix code on the block to make it appear to be original.

Point System

Our point system is a deduct scoring system. Please keep in mind that you are starting with a perfect slate and 4500 pts. One and two point deductions should not be of a great concern.

Maximum point loss to attain Awards:
See * qualifications below

All years
NCRS Top Flight	94-100%	maximum deduct 270 pts.
NCRS Second Flight	85-93.9%	maximum deduct 675 pts.
NCRS Third Flight	75-84.9%	maximum deduct 1125 pts.

* mileage points are added to raw score at the rate of 45 per 100 miles driven, up to 10% of your raw score maximum. The car must score at least 75% to be eligible for these points.

**Duntov/McLellan Award requires 97% raw score with no driving points added. Maximum deduction of 135 pts.

How to "Complain"

On-the-spot:

It is the judge's responsibility to explain why they made a deduction for a component. If you disagree with the reason, please feel free to explain any information that you believe the judge should be aware of that may change his mind. If after a short discussion, the judge does not change his decision, then we ask that you not "push" it any further. However, you may ask your team leader's opinion, and see if he would consider discussing your point further with the judge. If the team leader believes you have a valid point, he may further consult with the judges. Then if the judges decide to change their decision, the deduction will be changed on the score sheet. If the team leader believes you do not have a valid point, then we ask that you not "push" it any further. However, you may ask the National Judging Chairman or his representative his opinion and see if he would consider discussing your point further with the judges and team leader. If he believes you have a valid point, he may further consult with the judges. Then if the judges decide to change their decision, the deduction will be changed on the score sheet. In no case can anyone overrule the National Judging Chairman's decision. It is final.

After the show:

If still not satisfied with the decision, the owner may file a formal complaint in writing to David Brigham, NCRS National Judging Chairman, no later than thirty days after the date of the meet. The Chairman will personally review the case and provide the owner with an opinion of whether or not the judges were in error. Regardless of the findings (even if there was an error in judgment), no scores or certificates will be changed after the judging day, with the exception of an omission or a math error.

The reason for this policy is simple practicality. If every judging decision was open to debate, judging would require more personnel and time to administer than is available. Granted, mistakes can be made. However, we try to keep errors to a minimum and to give the benefit of doubt to the owner. Our track record has been remarkably good.

Disqualification

Late arrivals:

Any cars entered for judging not in place per the event requirements will be disqualified, with the exception of those who have experienced mechanical problems in route, and contacted the event judging chairman. He may extend their approved arrival time at his discretion.

Car Covers:

Car covers on all cars shall be removed no later than when judging starts, typically 8:00 AM, and remain off until at least 5:00 PM, while the cars are on the judging field. This includes all judged cars, even those being judged on a different day. This gives all members the opportunity to enjoy all the cars.

Early Departures:

All cars must remain on the judging field at least until the completion of judging the final day of judging. This includes NCRS Performance Verification cars and NCRS - Chevrolet Bowtie cars. NCRS Founders Award cars may be used for local transportation, provided it is done in an orderly manner with the event judging chairman's blessing, and there is no risk to surrounding cars or pedestrians. This is for safety purposes and will be strictly enforced.

Counterfeits:

Discovery of counterfeits (see Judging Reference Manual; section 2 Item 1) may subject owner to disqualification. In some cases, it might be in the best interest of the owner to withdraw his car from judging (see Judging Reference Manual; section 4 Item 12 Altered cars).

Conduct:

During the judging process, undesirable behavior by any member which threatens the intended friendly, family, hobby atmosphere of NCRS will not be tolerated
    NCRS judging consist of 4 teams of two judges on each team. The judges inspect (look at) each car for condition and originality of parts and equipment in the following areas: Operations, Chassis, Mechanical,

Interior, and Exterior. Check judging manual for more details. Each Corvette starts with 4510 points. Deductions are made for failure to meet condition and originality as called for in the judging manual.

Judging Information

Judging Score Sheets are now available for download at the www.NCRS.org

These sample sheets are made available so you can better understand the judging and scoring process. They are valuable for those preparing a car, and those preparing to judge or just refreshing your knowledge. These are PDF files for ease of viewing or printing your own copies. We will try to keep these up to date as future updates are made to the sheets. You will need the NCRS Technical Information Manual & Judging Guide for your car in order to utilize these sheets as they contain only point assignments and no component descriptions. You also should purchase the Judging Reference Manual as it contains all of the Standard Deductions that are used for certain items on the cars

National Corvette Restorers Society (NCRS)

NCRS judging consist of 4 teams of two judges on each team. The judges inspect (look at) each car for condition and originality of parts and equipment in the following areas: Operations, Chassis, Mechanical, Interior, and Exterior. Check judging manual for more details. Each Corvette starts with 4510 points. Deductions are made for failure to meet condition and originality as called for in the judging manual.

Top Flight Award

This award was created by the in 1974 to recognize cars that have been preserved or restored to the highest level of achievement through the NCRS Flight Judging Process. These cars have to achieve 94% or above of 4500 available points to earn "NCRS Top Flight" in a rigorous judging process of Operations Check, Exterior, Interior, Mechanical and Chassis Judging. As of today (30 October 2014) only 19,807 have gone through NCRS Flight Judging in attempting to earn this important mark of superiority, 14,613 have actually earned it.

Performance Verification (PV) Award

This award was created by the NCRS in 1985; the award recognizes individuals for the restoration and preservation of 1953 -1996 Corvettes. To achieve this award, an owner must attain a NCRS Flight award® based on an original "as manufactured" standard at a NCRS event; as well as present the car for a rigorous performance test of all vehicle mechanical components and functions, all of which must operate as those of a new car, without a single failure. As of today (30 October 2014) only 1,402 Corvettes have received the NCRS Performance Verification (PV) Award. Among the NCRS community the PV is commonly referred to as "The test that makes grown men cry".

ZORA ARKUS-DUNTOV Mark of Excellence Award

This award was created by the NCRS in 1985, in honor of Mr. Zora Arkus-Duntov, long-time Chief Engineer for the Chevrolet Corvette, who retired from General Motors in 1975. The Zora Arkus-Duntov Award recognizes individuals for the restoration and preservation of 1953-1974 Corvettes. To achieve this coveted award, an owner must attain a judging score of at least 97% out of 100% based on an original "as manufactured" standard at a National or Regional NCRS event; as well as present the car for a rigorous performance test of all vehicle mechanical components and functions, all of which must operate as those of a new car, without a single failure. Finally, the car must again score at least 97%, at a National NCRS Convention, to receive the Zora Arkus-Duntov Award. The process of achieving the Zora Arkus-Duntov Award requires attendance at a minimum of three events, and must be completed within a three year period. Only 978 Corvettes have achieved the NCRS Zora Arkus-Duntov Mark of Excellence Award.

Copyright © 2010 NCRS. Used with permission.

NCRS Flight Scoring System

Overall Scoring

The NCRS system is based on the deduction method of scoring. All cars begin the judging process with 4500 points. Whole-point deductions for those items whose operation or appearance fall outside our Judging Standard as determined by the various judging teams. At the completion of judging, the total points deducted are subtracted from 4500. The Bonus Scoring Points as outlined in Judging Reference Manual, Section 2, item #25 are added and the result is then divided by 45 to arrive at a total net score based on a 100-point system. These calculations are made to one decimal place and are not rounded up. For example, a calculated score of 93.978 would be listed as a 93.9 net score and noted as such on the score sheet and appropriate records. This score will also be the Grand Total Score unless driven mileage points have been earned by the owner as described under Driven Mileage Points, in which case these points expressed as a percentage will be added to the net score to arrive at the Final Grand Total Score.

Driven Mileage Points

To encourage driving, any car entered in Flight Judging which is driven by the owner or a family member to an event is eligible to receive additional points based on miles driven to the event so long as the car receives a minimum 75.0 net score. Mileage points are limited to 10% of net scoring.

Points are calculated using the actual mileage driven to the event as reported on the Judging Summary sheet by the owner. This mileage is multiplied by 1 % (.01). Using this number, and not rounding up, figures beyond the tenths place are dropped and the result is added to the net score to arrive at the final Grand Total Score, Grand Total cannot exceed 100. For example, a car driven 37 miles to an event would have .3 added; while a car driven 375 miles would have 3.7 points added.

Some calculated examples follow:

Net Score	Mileage	Mileage Points	Grand Total
87.8	435	4.3	92.1
87.8	1135	8.7 (10% Max)	96.5
93.8	50	0.5	94.3
72.8	138	0.0 (Under 75.0)	72.8
98.7	299	2.9	100
96.1	9	0.0 (.09)	96.1

Mileage Points Not Applicable

Mileage points are to be computed and added to the net score of any car driven to an event and judged (as described above), and Flight Awards will be presented reflecting those additional points. Mileage points, however, may not be counted toward either the 97.0 net prerequisite score, or the 97.0 net final score required of those cars attempting to achieve the NCRS Mark-of-Excellence Awards, as outlined in Section 7 and 8 of Judging Reference Manual.

Flight Ratings

The final Grand Total Score will be used to determine Flight Ratings and Awards:

Top Flight	94.0 or above
Second Flight	85.0 through 93.9
Third Flight	75.0 through 84.9

Scoring Areas

NCRS Score Sheets are divided into five sections: Operations, Interior, Exterior, Mechanical and Chassis. Ideally, individual Judging Teams of two persons will cover each of these areas; however, this may be modified to suit either the small size of a division or the limited number of available qualified judges as determined by the Meet Judging Chairman. With the possible exception of operations, one-man judging teams should be avoided.

Standard Deduction Tables

Contained in Section 4 of this manual are NCRS Standard Deduction Tables, which have been established to promote overall judging consistency on certain items. These tables address originality scoring and must be referred to and utilized in scoring.

Operations Scoring

The Operation Scoring Section includes judging of basic operational functions of the car as outlined on the score sheet and may allow partial-point deductions. These functions will be judged based on performance-as-designed and that which would be expected at the time of delivery to a purchaser. There is no provision for repair or adjustment on the field during Flight or Founders judging. It is recommended that both owners and judges review and utilize the appropriate NCRS Operations & Performance Verification Test Guide to better and more accurately prepare for this area of judging.

Matrix System Scoring - Overview

The Interior, Exterior, Mechanical & Chassis Sections are scored using a Matrix system whereby the judges first determine and score the apparent originality of a component part or area and then, if at least 10% of the available originality points remain, judge and score the existing condition of that part or area, thereby arriving at a total for each line item.

Originality Scoring

NCRS Originality Scoring is based on a part, component part, or area appearing to the judges to comply with our Judging Standard by using their knowledge, experience and available information contained in the Technical Information Manual & Judging Guide. This judging specifically does not mean a successfully judged part is the original factory-installed part, but does imply it appears as though it could be. Likewise, in judging the originality of an area, such as body paint, a successful judging does not mean the existing paint is that which was originally applied at the factory, but does imply it appears as though it could be. Generally, a component part judged to appear as a complete original item will receive full originality scoring credit, regardless of its condition.

All originality deductions for items not covered in Section 4, Standard Deduction Guidelines will be made because of discernible differences from original as defined by CDCIF. CDCIF shall be recognized as the process for determining the extent to which a component being judged conforms to our judging standard.

Originality

The extent to which a component being judged conforms to the judging standard, in the following areas:

- C Configuration - The manner, in which components are shaped, molded, cast or machined. Part number, casting mark/logo should be considered part of the configuration

- D Date - The degree to which the component date conforms to the logical sequence of manufacture and typically observed GM supply sourcing intervals. The date may be distinguished by means other than being stamped, cast, etc., into a component

- C Completeness - The degree to which the component is totally present

- I Installation - The degree to which the component is installed correctly

- F Finish - The degree to which the component surface finish, gloss, texture, color, tint and type conform to our judging standard

Once this difference has been noted, originality deductions are to be made based not on the fact that is a GM service replacement, a GM licensed reproduction or an aftermarket reproduction component. The item must be judged based on the overall degree of correctness as installed on a given car.

Assigned Originality & Condition Points

As an additional aid to judging consistency, NCRS Judging Score Sheets divide and assign portions of the originality and condition point totals to specific items in a given section. See Section 4, Standard Deduction Guidelines, Judging Reference Manual.

10% Originality Rule

In order for an item or area to be scored on condition, it must first be judged and scored on originality. If, after scoring, the remaining credit is less than 10% of the assigned originality points (deduction is greater than 90%), that item or area shall not be judged on condition and will be scored as a full deduction in the condition column. In judging line-item sections that cover several different parts, this will apply and affect those components so judged, individually.

Condition Scoring

NCRS Condition Scoring is based on a part, component part or area appearing to the judges to comply with our Judging Standard as it regards condition and will normally be judged without regard to originality. An exception would arise when part of an assembly is missing. A partial deduction would be taken on originality and subsequently, a partial deduction on Condition would also be taken since that part is unavailable to judge. Condition judging will encompass items such as:

Interior — Tears, cracks, age, scuffing or fading of any interior fabric item; paint fading, chips or scratches; plating pits or rust; stainless trim dents or scratches; plastic cracks or scuffs; instrument face fading, steering wheel cracks; the presence of stains.

Exterior — Paint fading, chips, scratches, cracks, scratches, discoloration, permanent water spotting; chrome pitting, scratches, dents, discoloration; stainless dents, scratches; emblem fading, tire wear or stains.

Mechanical & Chassis — Paint aging or chips; condition of chrome, zinc, cadmium and aluminum; bushings, spring liners, damaged components, rust and corrosion.

Crossover Scoring

Occasionally, judging situations may arise where it is difficult to determine whether a deduction should properly be made in the originality or condition column and subjective judgments may be required. Judging Teams should confer with their Team Leader for guidance and consistency in this area. Whatever the decision may be, the appropriate point deduction should remain the same, regardless of whether it is made in the originality or condition column, so it does not affect the overall score on that item or area.

Full or Major Deductions

In the case where a full or major deduction is being made, the judges should consult with their Team Leader for his information and concurrence. The Team Leader is to initial each full deduction adjacent to the scoring entry, and confirm a clear reason is written on the score sheet for that deduction.

Over/Under Restoration

Any item or area judged which appears to fall outside our Judging Standard is subject to deduction and may equally apply whether it is above or below that standard.

Deduction Scoring, Notation & Review

Upon reaching agreement on the scoring of each item, the Judging Team will mark the points deducted in the appropriate column. In the case where no deduction is being made, the Team will note such by using a slash (/) only, not a zero (0). Judges shall NOT add any figures to arrive at a score sheet total.

After scoring each line item, judges must make brief, legible notations indicating the reason for each deduction, particularly as it relates to originality. Following completion of judging by each individual Team, the judges will briefly review the score sheet with the owner, have him/her initial the sheet, as specifically outlined in Section 2, item #16 of Judging Reference Manual, and print their names on each sheet.

Team Leader Review & Tabulation

Immediately upon completion of judging and owner review, the Team will give the score sheet to the Team Leader for check-off and general review. Any illegible, missing or extraordinary scoring should be addressed and clarified at that time with the Judging Team. Following Team Leader review, the score sheets will be given to the Meet Judging Chairman, or as directed, and then submitted to Tabulation.

Score Sheet Return to Owner

Flight, Performance Verification and Founders Operations scoring sheets will be mailed to owners within two (2) weeks of an event. They are not to be returned at the event. Note: NCRS Bowtie scoring sheets are not returned to the owner.

Reference *NCRS Judging Reference Manual*, section 3, "NCRS Flight Scoring System"
Copyright © 2010 NCRS. Used with permission.

NCRS Standard Deduction Guidelines, Purpose & Use

As an aid to overall meet-to-meet divisional judging consistency, the following originality deduction tables and judging guidelines are listed as reference for use by the Judging Teams. As the listings cover over four decades of production, they are general in nature.

Should a conflict exist between the appropriate Technical Information Manual & Judging Guide and these Standard Deduction Guidelines contact the Team Leader for resolution.

Items or areas not specifically addressed in these Standard Deduction Guidelines should be addressed through our matrix judging process Section 3, items #8 and #9. They do not override section 2, item #25. In the case of confusion, the Team Leader should be consulted.

Any originality deduction in excess of 90% automatically requires that no condition judging will be done on that item and all assigned condition points for that item will be deducted.

Engine-Block Cylinder Cases

Judges and owners are additionally referred to Section 2, item #23 of the Judging Reference Manual regarding engine block cylinder case stamp pads, originality deductions to be judged in the following order:

A. Correct normally configured casting number and case configuration. If incorrect, deduct 350 points and do not judge or score casting date or stamp pad. (See note*)

B. If A is judged to be correct, judge for correctly configured casting date within six (6) months prior to car build date. If incorrect, deduct 175 points and do not judge or score stamp pad. (See note*)

C. If A & B are judged to be correct, judge for appropriate, normally configured engine plant stamping and engine assembly date or serial number and alpha prefix or suffix code which matches car as listed in the appropriate judging guide. (See note*)

The engine pad is assigned 50 originality points: 1953 through mid-1960, if engine plant stamping is judged incorrect, deduct 50 points. Mid-1960 & later if VIN derivative is judged incorrect, deduct 25 points; if engine assembly date suffix code is judged incorrect, deduct 25 points. (See note*)

Judge D regardless of scoring on C

D. Judge for absence of paint, dirt, rust or other condition which obscures engine pad and presence of normal factory production machining marks. If either is judged negatively, deduct 38 points. (See note*)

*Note: Each of the above listed items must be scored as full credit or full deduction; no partial deductions are allowed. This analysis allows for a six (6) month time span between cylinder case casting date, stamped engine assembly date and vehicle build date. This time frame allows for the exception rather than the rule as the average normal production time span has been found to usually be closer to two (2) or eight (8) weeks.

Batteries

No Originality Deduction: Original or original design reproduction (indiscernible as installed*) Delco as described in the appropriate year Technical Information Manual & Judging Guide, and if applicable, appropriate plant and date stamp for the vehicle.

Table of Originality Deductions:

- Deduct 10% — Battery appearing as above but with no appropriate plant or date stamping, if applicable
- Deduct 30% — Reproductions differing from original design and construction in minor detail
- Deduct 50% — Delco, correctly-sized service replacement with appropriate top or side-post configuration
- Deduct 100% — Originality & Condition for others

*Do not remove caps for inspection.

Tires

No Originality Deduction: Four (4) matching Original Equipment Manufacturer (OEM) tires as described in the appropriate year Technical Information Manual & Judging Guide, and one (1) matching or non-matching OEM spare tire.

A. 1953 through 1974 Table of Originality Deductions:

- Deduct 10% — OEM brand and size tires which differ from original only because of federally required Department of Transportation (DOT) markings
- Deduct 20% — OEM brand, type and size tires which differ slightly from original in design, construction, material, tread width, tread pattern, white (or colored) wall width, style lettering or pattern
- Deduct 30% — OEM brand, type and size tires which differ considerably from original in design, construction, material, tread width, tread pattern, white (or colored) wall width, style lettering or pattern
- Deduct 40% — non-OEM brand having correct size and sidewall specifications
- Deduct 60% — Current-day OEM brand, service-replacement size, bias- or radial-ply tires or current equivalent sizing designation and correct whitewall width
- Deduct 75% — As above, non-OEM brand
- Deduct 100% — Originality and Condition, all others or those with whitewall mounted inboard

B. 1975 and newer model year Table of Originality Deductions:

- Deduct 10% - OEM brand and size tires which differ from original only because of markings or other minor differences
- Deduct 20% - OEM brand, type and size tires which differ slightly from original in design, construction, material, tread width, tread pattern, style lettering or pattern
- Deduct 30% - OEM brand, type and size that differ considerably from original in design, construction, and material, tread width, tread pattern, style lettering or pattern
- Deduct 60% - OEM Brand tire that is of the extended mobility type (run flat) on a car that does not have WY5 in the list of RPOs on its Service Parts Identification Label or OEM brand but tire is not of the extended mobility type (run flat) on a car that does have WY5 of the list of RPOs on its Service Parts Identification Label
- Deduct 75 % - non-OEM brand
- Deduct 100 % - Originality and Condition, for incorrect size or those with white letters mounted inboard or outboard

Percentages shown in both tables are for five (5) matching tires; deduct an additional 20% for each non-matching road tire. Do not deduct for a non-matching spare, which appears as original.

Condition Scoring Note: If the condition of any tire, including spare, appears to constitute a potential safety hazard in the operation of the vehicle, such as deterioration, damage or excessive tread wear, condition deductions up to the full amount for that tire or all such tires must be made.

Windshields, Door Glass, Roof Panels, Plexiglass & Vinyl Windows

No Originality Deduction: OEM as described in the appropriate year Technical Information Manual & Judging Guide, dated within 12 months prior to vehicle assembly.

Table of Originality Deductions:

- Deduct 20%---As above, excepting only the date
- Deduct 30%---OEM brand, later service replacement style with correct tinting, if applicable
- Deduct 50%---OEM brand, with incorrectly configured tinting
- Deduct 90%---1953-62 tinted front or side glass; or 1953-96 non-OEM brand replacement(s) or any year added tinting (film, etc.)

The above 12-month timeframe allows for the exception rather than the rule. Most normal production time spans will usually fall within one (1) to six (6) months of vehicle build.

Condition Scoring Note: If the condition of the windshield appears to constitute a potential safety hazard in the operation of the vehicle, such as cracks or excessive pitting, condition point deductions up to the full amount for that item must be made.

Headlamps

No Originality Deduction: Full set of matching sealed beam units of correct brand and style for the year as described in each manual

Table of Originality Deductions:

Divide total assigned headlamp points by number of lamps on car to arrive at equal per-lamp value:

- Deduct 70% per lamp value for correct brand and style service replacement

- Deduct 100% per lamp value and related condition points for each incorrect brand or style lamp 1953 through 1973 model years do not have DOT markings. Headlamps, discernible by the DOT marking for these model years are a three (3) point deduction per car for a full set.

Stainless Steel or Aluminized Replacement Components

These are the minimum deductions for the use of detectable replacement parts which were not originally constructed of stainless or aluminized steel. Starting in 1984 the fuel lines, brake fluid lines, exhaust pipes and mufflers were originally constructed of stainless steel. The deduction may be larger if the component is not correctly configured. The percentages shown are those to be deducted from the amount assigned or assignable to the specific item(s) listed. For example, if exhaust pipes and mufflers are stainless but the clamps, brackets and hangers are correct, the three (3) correct items would receive no originality deduction.

Table of Originality Deductions:

- Deduct 25% — Any part that was not originally aluminized
- Deduct 50% — Any part that was not originally stainless steel

Altered Cars - Horsepower/Color/Interior

Change of Engine Horsepower: refer to item #1 of Judging Reference Manual section Engine-Block Cylinder Cases.

Change of Exterior Color: 100% originality deduction.

Variation of Exterior Color Paint Shade: 20% originality deduction.

Change of Interior Color or Fabric: 50% originality deduction on every item affected by the alteration. (An item exhibiting both color and fabric change would receive a 100% deduct for that item.)

Trim Tag or Service Parts Identification Label

Beginning with the model-year 1963, Corvettes were fitted with a trim tag, which noted, among other information, the exterior body color, interior trim color and fabric.

Beginning in late production model-year 1984, Corvettes were fitted with a Service Parts Identification label, which identifies all color and options of the car as it left the factory.

A Trim Tag/Service Parts Identification Label authenticity block is included on the Scoring Summary Sheet and the Judging Summary Sheet (the "Green Sheet"). The Team Leader must sign the authentication area of the signature block on both documents; a Team Leader signature in the rejection area of the signature block will result in the vehicle being "Branded Counterfeit" and appropriate action will be taken. See Judging Reference Manual, section 2, item # 34 Counterfeit Discovery Penalties

Cars appearing with trim information unusual for normal production, such as exterior paint noted as PRIME, will need to be shown in that finish in order to comply with NCRS Judging Standards and suffer no automatic color change deduction. In the case of an exterior paint code such as SPEC. or SPECIAL, which usually denotes primer or a non-production color, it will the sole responsibility of the owner to provide satisfactory documentation to the judges confirming the color or finish applied at the factory, *not by the dealer*, or the deduction under color change will apply.

Added or Deleted Options

The detectable addition OR deletion of any regular production vehicle option subsequent to factory assembly is inconsistent with NCRS Judging Standards and therefore subject to a full deduction on originality and condition. Examples: power top, windshield washers, power windows, power steering, power brakes, side-mounted exhaust. Refer to NCRS Performance Verification Judging & Award, Section 6, item #3 Judging Purpose & Standard, pertaining to option addition or deletion.

Body Color

No Originality Deduction – Color corresponds to the factory-installed body trim plate color code, if applicable. The shade and the metallic content and/or size (if applicable) are consistent with that applied at the factory.

Deduct 20% of Originality – Color corresponds to the factory-installed body trim plate color code (if applicable). However, the color shade is not consistent with the color shade applied at the factory.

Deduct 50% of Originality – Color corresponds to the factory-installed body trim plate color code (if applicable). However, the metallic content and/or size (if applicable) is not consistent with the metallic content/size applied at the factory.

Deduct 100% of Originality – Color of side panel cove depression, hood stinger, and/or hardtop is a non-factory color, an unavailable factory color combination or applied to an inappropriate year of manufacture.

Deduct 100% of Originality – Color does not correspond to the factory-installed body trim plate color code (if applicable) or is a non-factory color or is a factory color applied in to inappropriate year of manufacture.

Body Paint

No Originality Deduction – The body paint is the original factory-applied finish or appears to have been refinished with the appropriate factory-applied material and appears consistent with factory application methods. Judge Condition separately.

Deduct 20% of Originality - for either A or B below. All Corvettes were produced under assembly-line conditions subject to established acceptable manufacturing conditions and tolerances.

- A. The body paint appears to have been refinished with the appropriate factory-applied material; however, the degree of coverage is inconsistent with factory application methods. Body paint is evident on weather strip or trim, which was applied after the factory applied paint. Judge Condition separately.

- B. Over/Under Restoration – Evaluate body paint for over/under restoration. Factory applied body paint typically has evidence of orange peel or overspray in areas that are typical for that year of application. Finishes that exceed typical factory standards shall receive deduction. Judge Condition separately.

Deduct 50% of Originality – The body paint appears to have been refinished with a material not consistent with factory application but the appearance is consistent with factory application methods. Judge Condition separately.

Deduct 100% of Originality and Condition – for either A or B below

A. The body paint appears to have been refinished with a material not consistent with factory application and the appearance is not consistent with factory application methods. Total deduction for Originality and Condition.

B. The presence of *any* custom paint modifications which shall include lettering (any media), pin striping, race car numbers, race style stripes, flames or any other non-factory inspired additions. Total deduction for Originality and Condition.

Body Fiberglass and Component Fit

No Originality Deduction – The body appears to be as assembled by the factory from originally manufactured components. Body panels are of appropriate color and finish on both sides with bonding strips, if applicable, at the appropriate locations. Panel alignment of doors, hood, trunk, etc. is within acceptable factory tolerances. Judge Condition separately.

Deduct 20% of Originality – Over/Under Restoration – All Corvettes were produced under assembly line conditions subject to established acceptable manufacturing conditions and tolerances. Evaluate panel alignment and surface finish for over/under restoration. Panel smoothness and gap dimensions that exceed factory tolerances shall receive deduction. Judge Condition separately.

Deduct 40% of Originality – The presence of an inappropriate hood for either year or engine application. This includes all hoods not typical of factory manufacture. Judge Condition separately.

Deduct 50% of Originality – The presence of a one-piece front end with bonding strips in appropriate factory locations. Judge Condition separately.

Deduct 80% of Originality – The presence of a one-piece front end without bonding strips. Judge Condition separately.

Deduct 100% of Originality and Condition – The presence of any custom body modifications or an original Corvette body mated with an inconsistent Vehicle Identification Number (VIN). Total deduction for Originality and Condition.

GM-Service Replacement, GM-Licensed Reproduction Parts and Non-OEM Parts

There is a wide variation in original versus later issue versus present-day configuration of items listed and sold by GM as service replacement, GM-licensed reproduction and non-OEM parts. It is therefore difficult to place a consistent, fair deduction on each item. All parts that are correct and indiscernible from original as installed will receive no originality deduction even though a judge may know, or thinks he/she knows, they are not original components. There can be no deduction because a judge thinks an item looks *too new* to be an original item. See Judging Reference Manual, Section 3, item #9.

Originality deductions are to be made based not on the fact that is a GM-service replacement, a GM licensed reproduction or non-OEM component. The item must be judged based on the overall degree of correctness as installed on a given car.

Parts that appear reasonably correct as installed will be evaluated for originality (and possible deduction) per CDCIF section 3, item #9.

Parts that are significantly dissimilar as installed will receive a Standard Deduction of 100% for Originality per Judging Reference Manual, Section 3, item #14. Team Leader concurrence is required.

GM-Approved Dealer-Installed Accessories

Because of conflict with the NCRS Judging Standard, a small deduction will be made for any Chevrolet dealer-installed accessory, such as a luggage rack, right-hand rearview mirror, etc., which was not available through the Corvette assembly plant, even though such an item was approved, sold and installed by the dealer as a General Motors part. These items are limited only to those listed in Chevrolet literature as being specifically available for the Corvette that are correct for the model year on which they appear, if they are installed to General Motors specifications.

Proof of availability will rest with the owner. In making the point deduction, the judge will take into consideration the extent to which the addition of the accessory alters the component or subassembly to which the accessory is affixed. For example, the addition of a dealer-installed luggage rack results in holes in the rear deck fiberglass area. Point deductions for the missing fiberglass will be scored on the appropriate line item of the exterior score sheet. The amount of points deducted for these items may be specified in the respective Technical Information Manual & Judging Guide.

Factory Recall Modification

Owners able to document Chevrolet notice for a factory recall modification to their vehicles and that appears to have been performed by a Chevrolet Dealer to factory specifications will receive a minimum originality deduction.

Reference *NCRS Judging Reference Manual*, section 4, "NCRS Standard Deduction Guidelines, Purpose & Use" Copyright © 2010 NCRS. Used with permission.

NCRS 1963-1967 SCORING SUMMARY

(Revised 11/2002)

Owner's Name: _____ Membership #: _____ Date: _____
Address: _____
City: _____ State: _____ Zip: _____
Area Code & Phone: _____
Chapter Affiliation (if any): _____
Location of Meet: _____

☐ Chapter   ☐ Regional   ☐ National Convention

Model Year: _____ Complete VIN: _____ Horsepower: _____
Exterior Color: _____ Interior Color: _____ Fabric: _____

☐ Coupe   ☐ Convertible
☐ Driven _____ Miles   ☐ Trailered _____ Miles

SCORING SUMMARY SECTION

Team Leader Trim Tag Sub Section

Rejection Signature _____

Printed name _____ **Authentication Signature *** _____

__The highest award available without the above Team Leader Signature, here and on the Judging Summary Sheet (Green Sheet) will be a Second Flight Award regardless of the Grand Total Score.__

Transfer to Judging Summary Sheet (Green Sheet).

Operations Section (760 possible w/bonus) .... _____

Interior Section (790 possible) .... _____

Exterior Section (1020 possible) .... _____

Mechanical Section (1240 possible) .... _____

Chassis Section (700 possible) .... _____

Total RAW Score (4510 possible) .... _____

Net Score (Divide Raw score by 45 figure to 1/10th do not round .... _____

Driving Points (Refer to Reference Manual) 100% is the maximum score attainable .... _____

* Grand Total Score .... _____

Judging Chairman Signature _____   Tab Initial _____

Flight Award Presented   * Top 94 ☐   2nd 85 ☐   3rd 75 ☐   None ☐

Flight Scoring System NCRS 1963–1967 Scoring Summary Sheet
Copyright © NCRS. Used with permission.

NCRS 1963-1967
Operations
Page 1 of 2 *Revised 11/02*

Name _____
VIN _____
Model _____ Year _____

Scoring: Deduct 25 points for each line item failure. Make partial deductions for faulty or incomplete function. If no deduction or if not so equipped (or appropriate to year and model), mark with a diagonal slash. If deduction is made, note reason for deduction to right of the judged item. No repair or adjustment during judging.

Score   Reason for deduction

A. Performed by Team Leader
☐ VIN plate authenticity & attachment

B. Performed by Operations Judging Team
Start judging with a cold engine for proper testing of choke operation. Start engine with hood open and with air cleaner in place. Ensure car is in neutral or park with parking brake set.

Score   Reason for Deduction

1. ☐ Ease of start
       (score choke & idle at item 18)
2. ☐ Horns & horn button contact
       (rotate headlights to open position)
3. ☐ Headlights - high & low beam
       (rotate headlights to closed position)
4. ☐ Headlight motor operation
5. ☐ Park lights, front & rear
6. ☐ License light & taillights
7. ☐ Brake light & back-up lights
8. ☐ Turn signal lights & hazard
9. ☐ Windshield washer
10. ☐ Windshield wipers - 2 speeds
11. ☐ High beam & turn indicators
12. ☐ Headlight & park brake warning indicators
        note: 1967 parking brake indicator light does not flash
13. ☐ Gauges & tachometer operation
14. ☐ Antenna operation
15. ☐ Radio operation
16. ☐ Heater, defroster & air condition operation
17. ☐ Kick panel vents & rear exhaust vent

For tabulation use only
Deduction subtotal, page 1 of 2
Tabulator initial ____ ____

NCRS 1963–1967 Operations Scoring Sheets (1 of 2)
Copyright © NCRS. Used with permission.

NCRS 1963-1967
Operations
Page 2 of 2 *Revised 11/02*

Name _____
VIN _____
Model _____ Year _____

18. ☐ Choke: fast & slow idle
19. ☐ Exhaust: tone, leakage, noise
20. ☐ Engine noises & vibration: fan clutch, lifters
21. ☐ Leaks: water, fuel, oil, brake fluid
22. ☐ Reverse lock-out or neutral safety switch & park brake function
Stop engine
23. ☐ Clock & reset function
24. ☐ Cigarette lighter & well
25. ☐ Lights: courtesy, rear compartment or dome, glove compartment
26. ☐ Lights & brightness control: dash, gauge, ignition & radio
27. ☐ Odometer reset function & tele-column function
28. ☐ Seat adjustment, back latching, seat belts & retractors
29. ☐ Windows: side & vent operation
30. ☐ Locking & latching: glove compartment, ignition, doors & spare tire

Bonus Points
Yes ☐ No ☐   Fire extinguisher   3 point bonus
Yes ☐ No ☐   Battery disconnect switch   3 point bonus
Yes ☐ No ☐   NCRS window decal   3 point bonus

Review
Judge _____   Judge _____
Owner review & initial ____   Team Leader review & initial ____   Judging Chairman review & initial ____

For tabulation use only
Deduction subtotal, page 2 of 2
Tabulator initial ____

For tabulation use only
Page 1 subtotal = ____   Tabulator initial ____
Page 2 subtotal = ____   750
Total deduction ____   (Subtract from 750 possible) -
                                    Subtotal ____
Bonus points: Add 3 points for each "yes" (10 points if all "yes")
                           Total Operations ____
Transfer score to Scoring Summary & Judging Summary Sheets

NCRS 1963–1967 Operations Scoring Sheets (2 of 2)
Copyright © NCRS. Used with permission.

NCRS 1963-1967 Mechanical
Page 1 of 4 Revised 11/02

Name: _____
VIN: _____
Model: _____ Year _____

Engine Code: _____ Horsepower: _____

Scoring: Point assignments at left of score boxes. Mark originality deductions in first column and condition deductions in second column. If no deduction, mark score box with a diagonal slash. If deduction is made, note reason for deduction to right of the judged item.

Score
Originality | Condition | Reason for deduction

1. Engine Color, Paint & Mounts Originality: 25 Condition: 25 Total: 50
- 20 | 20 | Engine color & paint
- 5 | 5 | Front engine mounts & ground strap

2. Cylinder Case Originality: 350 Condition: none Total: 350
- 350 | none | A. Casting number & case configuration
  (if incorrect, deduct 350 & do not judge or score B, C or D below)
- 175 | none | B. Casting date
  (if incorrect, deduct 175 & do not judge or score C or D below)
- 25 | none | C. Assembly stamping
- 25 | none | VIN derivative
- 38 | none | D. Stamp pad surface finish

3. Cylinder Heads Originality: 50 Condition: none Total: 50
- 50 | none | Cylinder heads

4. Valve Covers Originality: 25 Condition: 25 Total: 50
- 16 | 16 | Valve covers
- 4 | 4 | Attachment & clips
- 5 | 5 | Decals, stickers & gaskets

5. Air Cleaner *(Judge A Or B Only, Check Box)* Originality: 30 Condition: 30 Total: 60
- **A. Carbureted Cars** ☐
- 20 | 20 | Air cleaner assembly
- 5 | 5 | Element
- 5 | 5 | Attachment, labels, hoses & clamps
- **B. Fuel Injected Cars** ☐
- 25 | 25 | Air cleaner & instruction
- 5 | 5 | Air hose & clamps

For tabulation use only
☐ + ☐ = ☐ Deduction subtotal, page 1 of 4
Tabulator initial ☐ ☐

NCRS 1963–1967 Mechanical Scoring Sheets (1 of 4)
Copyright © NCRS. Used with permission.

NCRS 1963-1967 Mechanical
Page 2 of 4 Revised 11/02

Name: _____
VIN: _____
Model: _____ Year _____

6. Fuel System & Intake Manifold *(Judge A Or B Only, Check Box)*
- **A. Carbureted Cars** ☐ Originality: 70 Condition: 50 Total: 120
- 40 | 20 | Carburetor
- 25 | 25 | Intake manifold, bolts, gaskets & seals
- 5 | 5 | Thermostat housing & attachment
- **B. Fuel Injected Cars** ☐ Originality: 71 Condition: 49 Total: 120
- 60 | 40 | FI Unit, drive cable, base plate, bolts, gaskets & seals
- 3 | 2 | Plenum ID tag
- 3 | 2 | Fuel meter ID tag
- 5 | 5 | Thermostat housing & attachment

7. Accelerator Lever & Linkage Originality: 15 Condition: 15 Total: 30
- 5 | 5 | Accelerator lever on firewall
- 10 | 10 | Linkage, brackets, springs & ground strap

8. Oil Fill System Originality: 10 Condition: 10 Total: 20
- 10 | 10 | Oil fill tube, hose & cap

9. Fuel Delivery System Originality: 28 Condition: 22 Total: 50
- 15 | 10 | Fuel pump
- 8 | 8 | Engine compartment: lines, fittings & clamps
- 5 | 4 | Fuel filter & attachment (if equipped)

10. Ignition System & Shields Originality: 45 Condition: 35 Total: 80
- 10 | 10 | Heat & radio shielding, grounds & brackets
- 5 | 5 | Ignition coil, mounting & capacitor
- 15 | 10 | Distributor, cap & vacuum advance
- 10 | 5 | Spark plugs & wires
- 2 | 2 | Tachometer drive cable
- 3 | 3 | Transistor ignition, harness & amplifier (all 396 & if equipped)

For tabulation use only
☐ + ☐ = ☐ Deduction subtotal, page 2 of 4
Tabulator initial ☐ ☐

NCRS 1963-1967 Mechanical Scoring Sheets (2 of 4)
Copyright © NCRS. Used with permission.

NCRS 1963-1967 Mechanical — Page 3 of 4

Revised 11/02

Name _____ VIN _____ Model _____ Year _____

11. Exhaust Manifold & A.I.R. — Originality: 30 Condition: 30 Total: 60

Orig.	Cond.	Item
15	15	Manifolds
5	5	Bolts, studs, nuts, flanges, locks, washers & heat riser
10	10	A.I.R. system - all (if equipped)

12. Engine Oil — Originality: 13 Condition: 12 Total: 25

Orig.	Cond.	Item
6	6	Oil dipstick
4	4	Dipstick tube
3	2	Pressure line assembly (to gauge & FI distributor)

13. Water Pumping System — Originality: 26 Condition: 24 Total: 50

Orig.	Cond.	Item
6	4	Water pump & fittings
5	5	Radiator hoses & clamps
2	2	By-pass hose & clamps (if equipped)
5	5	Heater hoses, clamps & clips
4	4	Balancer & pulleys: Crankshaft, water pump & idler assembly
4	4	Fan belt(s) - all

14. Alternator — Originality: 25 Condition: 15 Total: 40

Orig.	Cond.	Item
15	11	Alternator - model & date
5	2	Pulley & fan
5	2	Mounting, adjusting brackets & hardware

15. Battery & Cables — Originality: 40 Condition: 25 Total: 65

Orig.	Cond.	Item
25	15	Battery & caps
8	5	Battery cables, felt washer & clips
7	5	Tray, hold-down, shield & retaining hardware

16. Electrical — Originality: 28 Condition: 22 Total: 50

Orig.	Cond.	Item
8	7	Engine compartment & Back-up light wiring harnesses include all blocks
4	4	Wiring clips & retainers
7	5	Voltage regulator & capacitor
6	4	Horn relay
3	2	Ballast resistor

For tabulation use only
___ + ___ = Deduction subtotal, page 3 of 4
Tabulator initial ___

NCRS 1963-1967 Mechanical — Page 4 of 4

Revised 11/02

Name _____ VIN _____ Model _____ Year _____

17. Heating or Air Conditioning — Originality: 27 Condition: 18 Total: 45

Orig.	Cond.	Item
4	3	Heater box & fan motor or block-off plate
5	3	Compressor assembly, mounting & labels
3	2	Evaporator, relay & label
5	3	Valves
2	2	Hoses, pipes, clamps & grommets
3	2	Dehydrator assembly
5	3	Condenser

18. Wiper & Washer System — Originality: 13 Condition: 12 Total: 25

Orig.	Cond.	Item
6	6	Wiper motor
3	3	Washer pump, hoses & clips
4	3	Reservoir, fluid & brackets

19. Overall Cleanliness — Originality: none Condition: 20 Total: 20

Orig.	Cond.	Item
none	20	Overall cleanliness of items 1-18

Review

Judge _____ Judge _____

Owner review & initial ___ Team Leader review & initial ___ Judging Chairman review & initial ___

For tabulation use only
___ + ___ = Deduction subtotal, page 4 of 4
Tabulator initial ___

For tabulation use only
Page 1 subtotal = ___
Page 2 subtotal = ___
Page 3 subtotal = ___
Page 4 subtotal = ___
Total deduction = ___

Tabulator initial ___

1240 (subtract from 1240 possible) - ___
Total Mechanical ___

Transfer score to Scoring Summary & Judging Summary Sheets

NCRS 1963–1967 Mechanical Scoring Sheets (3 of 4)
Copyright © NCRS. Used with permission.

NCRS 1963–1967 Mechanical Scoring Sheets (4 of 4)
Copyright © NCRS. Used with permission.

NCRS 1963-1967 Interior
Page 1 of 4   *Revised 11/02*

Name _____
VIN _____
Model _____ Year _____

Scoring: Point assignments at left of score boxes. Mark originality deductions in first column and condition deductions in second column. If no deduction, mark score box with a diagonal slash. If deduction is made, note reason for deduction to right of the judged item.

Score
Originality   Condition   Reason for deduction

1. Door Panel Area   Originality: 36   Condition: 34   Total: 70
17	15	Door panels
5	5	Panel trim & pulls
4	4	Window cranks
4	4	Door release & locking knobs
3	3	Window surround trim
3	3	Interior window seals

2. Door Opening Area   Originality: 25   Condition: 25   Total: 50
4	4	Body jambs
4	4	Courtesy light switch & hinges
4	4	Sill plates
2	2	Strikers
6	6	Door jambs & latches
5	5	Weatherstripping

3. Interior Roof Area   (Judge A, B or C only, Check Box)   Originality: 26   Condition: 24   Total: 50

A. Coupe ☐
16	14	Headliner & halo panel
8	8	Trim moldings
2	2	Rear compartment bulkhead vinyl

B. Convertible with soft top ☐
7	5	Interior of top
6	6	Top frame
5	5	Header latches & strikers
5	5	Rear deck latches
3	3	Deck underside

☐ + ☐ = ☐   *For tabulation use only*
Deduction subtotal, page 1 of 4
Tabulator initial

NCRS 1963–1967 Interior Scoring Sheets (1 of 4)
Copyright © NCRS. Used with permission.

NCRS 1963-1967 Interior
Page 2 of 4   *Revised 11/02*

Name _____
VIN _____
Model _____ Year _____

3. Interior Roof Area (continued)   (Judge A, B or C only, Check Box)
Originality: 26   Condition: 24   Total: 50

C. Convertible with hardtop ☐
10	8	Headliner
5	5	Trim moldings
5	5	Header latches & strikers
3	3	Hardtop to rear deck attachment
3	3	Deck underside

4. Windshield Trim   Originality: 27   Condition: 23   Total: 50
10	8	Interior rear view mirror
7	7	Windshield interior trim
10	8	Sunshades & attaching hardware

5. Dash Panel Area   Originality: 27   Condition: 23   Total: 50
2	2	Dash panel
4	4	Defroster outlet trim & speaker grille
3	3	Side trim panels
2	2	Attachment tabs & rivets
12	8	Dash pads
4	4	Air conditioning vents (if equipped)

6. Instruments   Originality: 40   Condition: 35   Total: 75
5	5	Cluster housing
20	20	Instruments, faces & lenses
5	5	Clock: Housing, face & lens
10	5	Radio: Housing, face, lens, buttons & antenna switch (1965 & 66 only)

7. Glove Compartment   Originality: 21   Condition: 19   Total: 40
8	6	Door assembly & label (1966 & 67 only)
4	4	Compartment interior
5	5	Contents
4	4	Light & shield, lock & latch

☐ + ☐ = ☐   *For tabulation use only*
Deduction subtotal, page 2 of 4
Tabulator initial

NCRS 1963–1967 Interior Scoring Sheets (2 of 4)
Copyright © NCRS. Used with permission.

NCRS 1963-1967 Interior — Page 3 of 4
Revised 11/02

Name _____
VIN _____
Model _____ Year _____

8. Controls — Originality: 25 | Condition: 25 | Total: 50

Orig	Cond	Item
3	3	Ignition switch
12	12	Knobs & lighter
2	2	Fresh air pulls & fan control for 64 & 65 coupes
2	2	Trip odometer
2	2	Hood release
2	2	Headlight motor switch
2	2	Parking brake handle

9. Steering — Originality: 20 | Condition: 20 | Total: 40

Orig	Cond	Item
10	10	Steering wheel & horn button
3	3	Turn signal lever
4	4	Steering column & telescopic release (if equipped)
3	3	Hazard flasher switch (1966 & 67 only)

10. Console Area — Originality: 36 | Condition: 24 | Total: 60

Orig	Cond	Item
9	5	Console, shift pattern & power window switch (if equipped)
15	10	Shifter, knob & boot
2	2	Ashtray
2	2	Seat belt retainers (1965, 66 & 67 only)
8	5	Cushion (1963-66 only) or parking brake cover (1967 only)

11. Seating Area — Originality: 50 | Condition: 40 | Total: 90

Orig	Cond	Item
24	16	Seats, backs & trim
4	4	Adjusting levers & back latch (1967 only)
4	4	Frames & tracks
14	12	Seat belts, tags & belt buckles
4	4	Belt retractors, boots & anchor plates

12. Rear Storage Area — Originality: 25 | Condition: 20 | Total: 45

Orig	Cond	Item
6	6	Storage cover underside, labels & instruction & thumb hole bezel
3	3	Storage compartments
16	11	Jack, jack retainer, wheel wrench & associated tools

For tabulation use only
____ + ____ = Deduction subtotal, page 3 of 4
Tabulator initial ____

NCRS 1963–1967 Interior Scoring Sheets (3 of 4)
Copyright © NCRS. Used with permission.

NCRS 1963-1967 Interior — Page 4 of 4
Revised 11/02

Name _____
VIN _____
Model _____ Year _____

13. Carpet Area — Originality: 33 | Condition: 27 | Total: 60

Orig	Cond	Item
13	11	Carpet color & weave
6	3	Seams, binding & fit
4	2	Heel pad & dimmer switch grommet
4	4	Kick panels
3	3	Air vent grilles
4	4	Rear quarter trim panels

14. Under Dash Area — Originality: 20 | Condition: 20 | Total: 40

Orig	Cond	Item
6	6	Pedals & pads
5	5	Fuse panel & wiring
2	2	Firewall insulation
2	2	Courtesy lights
2	2	Signal flasher & capacitor & 67 hazard flasher
3	3	Heater assembly

15. Overall Cleanliness — Originality: none | Condition: 20 | Total: 20

Orig	Cond	Item
none	20	Overall cleanliness of items 1-14

Review

Judge _____ Judge _____

Owner review & initial ____
Team Leader review & initial ____
Judging Chairman review & initial ____

For tabulation use only
____ + ____ = Deduction subtotal, page 4 of 4
Tabulator initial ____

For tabulation use only
Page 1 subtotal = ____
Page 2 subtotal = ____
Page 3 subtotal = ____
Page 4 subtotal = ____
Total deduction ____ (subtract from 790 possible) - 790
Total Interior ____
Tabulator initial ____

Transfer score to Scoring Summary & Judging Summary Sheets

NCRS 1963–1967 Interior Scoring Sheets (4 of 4)
Copyright © NCRS. Used with permission.

NCRS 1963-1967 Exterior — Page 1 of 4

Revised 11/02

Name: _____
VIN: _____
Model: _____ Year: _____

Scoring: Point assignments at left of score boxes. Mark originality deductions in first column and condition deductions in second column. If no deduction, mark score box with a diagonal slash. If deduction is made, note reason for deduction to right of the judged item.

1. Body Color — Originality: 85, Condition: none, Total: 85
- 85 / none — Body color (refer to Judging Reference Manual, Section 4 #12)

2. Body Paint — Originality: 45, Condition: 40, Total: 85
- 45 / 40 — Body paint

3. Body Fiberglass & Component Fit — Originality: 65, Condition: 55, Total: 120
- 65 / 55 — Fiberglass & component fit

4. Top (Judge A, B or C only, Check Box) — Originality: 35, Condition: 35, Total: 70

A. Coupe ☐
- 20 / 20 — Rear glass, logo & date
- 10 / 10 — Trim
- 5 / 5 — Vent grilles (1964 & 65 only)

B. Convertible with soft top ☐
- 10 / 10 — Color & material
- 7 / 7 — Stitching & binding
- 16 / 16 — Rear window, logo & date
- 2 / 2 — Warning label

C. Convertible with hardtop ☐
- 8 / 8 — Exterior trim
- 20 / 20 — Rear window, logo & date
- 7 / 7 — Weatherstrip & side window seals

5. Windshield & Trim — Originality: 30, Condition: 30, Total: 60
- 20 / 20 — Windshield logo & date
- 10 / 10 — Trim & gasket

6. Side Glass & Trim — Originality: 15, Condition: 15, Total: 30
- 5 / 5 — Vent glass & trim
- 10 / 10 — Side glass & trim

For tabulation use only
☐ + ☐ = ☐ Deduction subtotal, page 1 of 4
Tabulator initial ☐ ☐

NCRS 1963–1967 Exterior Scoring Sheets (1 of 4)
Copyright © NCRS. Used with permission.

NCRS 1963-1967 Exterior — Page 2 of 4

Revised 11/02

Name: _____
VIN: _____
Model: _____ Year: _____

7. Wipers & Cowl — Originality: 20, Condition: 20, Total: 40
- 4 / 4 — Wiper arms
- 8 / 8 — Wiper blades & holders
- 5 / 5 — Cowl area & grilles
- 3 / 3 — Washer nozzles & tubing

8. Emblems & Trim — Originality: 25, Condition: 20, Total: 45
- 5 / 5 — Front nose emblem
- 8 / 5 — Hood: Grilles, script and/or trim
- 7 / 5 — Side emblems
- 5 / 5 — Rear deck script

9. Fuel Filler Area — Originality: 10, Condition: 10, Total: 20
- 5 / 5 — Fuel door, bezel & emblem
- 2 / 2 — Boot & overflow hose
- 3 / 3 — Fuel cap

10. Radio Antenna — Originality: 10, Condition: 10, Total: 20
- 10 / 10 — Antenna assembly

11. Mirror & Door Handles — Originality: 15, Condition: 15, Total: 30
- 9 / 9 — Exterior mirror
- 6 / 6 — Door handles, key lock bezel & gasket

12. Headlight Area — Originality: 20, Condition: 10, Total: 30
- 8 / 7 — Housings, covers & light bezels
- 12 / 3 — Headlights (3 points per bulb)

13. Front Bumper Area — Originality: 20, Condition: 20, Total: 40
- 10 / 10 — Front bumpers
- 4 / 4 — Bumper braces & bolts
- 3 / 3 — Bumper bar
- 3 / 3 — License bracket & frame

14. Grille — Originality: 15, Condition: 15, Total: 30
- 15 / 15 — Grille, mounting brackets, supports & braces

For tabulation use only
☐ + ☐ = ☐ Deduction subtotal, page 2 of 4
Tabulator initial ☐ ☐

NCRS 1963–1967 Exterior Scoring Sheets (2 of 4)
Copyright © NCRS. Used with permission.

NCRS 1963-1967
Exterior
Page 3 of 4   Revised 11/02

Name _____
VIN _____
Model _____ Year _____

15. Front Parking Lights		Originality: 10	Condition: 10	Total: 20
10	10	Light assemblies (5 points each)		

16. Rocker Moldings or Covers		Originality: 15	Condition: 15	Total: 30
15	15	Molding or side exhaust covers, brackets & fasteners		

17. Rear License Area		Originality: 20	Condition: 20	Total: 40
3	3	License bezel & frame		
3	3	License light		
10	10	Taillight and/or backup lights		
4	4	Exhaust bezels		

18. Rear Bumpers		Originality: 15	Condition: 15	Total: 30
10	10	Rear bumpers		
3	3	Bumper braces & bolts		
2	2	Rear valance panel attachment		

19. Spare Tire Stowage		Originality: 13	Condition: 12	Total: 25
3	2	Spare tire lock, boot & key		
5	5	Spare tire housing		
5	5	Spare tire carrier & bolts		

20. Tires		Originality: 30	Condition: 30	Total: 60
30	30	Tires - including spare		

21. Wheels & Wheel covers	(Judge A or B only, Check Box)	Originality: 40	Condition: 35	Total: 75
A. Standard Wheels	☐			
25	20	Steel wheels, weights, valve stems & caps		
10	10	Wheel covers or Rally trim rings		
5	5	Spinners or Rally hubcaps		
B. Optional wheels	☐ (1964-67 only)			
30	25	Aluminum wheels, weights, valve stems & caps		
10	10	Spinners or Rally hubcaps		

For tabulation use only
☐ + ☐ = ☐ Deduction subtotal, page 3 of 4
Tabulator initial ☐ ☐

NCRS 1963–1967 Exterior Scoring Sheets (3 of 4)
Copyright © NCRS. Used with permission.

NCRS 1963-1967
Exterior
Page 4 of 4   Revised 11/02

Name _____
VIN _____
Model _____ Year _____

22. Wheel wells		Originality: 8	Condition: 7	Total: 15
8	7	Wheel wells & undercoating		

23. Overall Cleanliness		Originality: none	Condition: 20	Total: 20
none	20	Overall cleanliness of items 1 - 22		

Review

Judge _____   Judge _____

Owner review & initial ☐   Team Leader review & initial ☐   Judging Chairman review & initial ☐

For tabulation use only
☐ + ☐ = ☐ Deduction subtotal, page 4 of 4
Tabulator initial ☐ ☐

For tabulation use only
Page 1 subtotal = ☐
Page 2 subtotal = ☐   Tabulator initial ☐ ☐
Page 3 subtotal = ☐
Page 4 subtotal = ☐   1020
Total deduction ☐ (subtract from 1020 possible) - 1020
Total Exterior ☐
Transfer score to Scoring Summary & Judging Summary Sheets

NCRS 1963–1967 Exterior Scoring Sheets (4 of 4)
Copyright © NCRS. Used with permission.

NCRS 1963-1967 Chassis
Page 1 of 4 — Revised 11/02

Name _____ VIN _____ Model _____ Year _____

Scoring: Point assignments at left of score boxes. Mark originality deductions in first column and condition deductions in second column. If no deduction, mark score box with a slash. If deduction is made, note reason for deduction to right of the judged item.

Engine Code _____ Horsepower _____

Score Originality	Condition		Reason for deduction

1. Brake System — Originality: 22 Condition: 18 Total: 40

12	8	Master cylinder & cap
5	5	Power brake booster & hose
5	5	Engine compartment: valves, lines, fittings & clips

2. Steering — Originality: 20 Condition: 20 Total: 40

3	3	Steering column & shaft
6	6	Coupler (rag joint) assembly
3	3	Steering gear box
8	8	Power steering: pump, pulleys, valve, bracket & hoses

3. Engine Compartment — Originality: 30 Condition: 25 Total: 55

20	15	Inner fenders, firewall, blackout & sealing
3	3	Dust shields & staples
4	4	Upper A arms & shock attachment
3	3	Splash shields & weatherstripping

4. Hood & Hardware — Originality: 20 Condition: 15 Total: 35

6	4	Configuration, blackout & paint margin
3	3	Weatherstrip & trim attachment
5	4	Hinges & hood support
6	4	Hood catches, pins & associated hardware

For tabulation use only
☐ + ☐ = ☐ Deduction subtotal, page 1 of 4
Tabulator initial ☐ ☐

NCRS 1963–1967 Chassis Scoring Sheets (1 of 4)
Copyright © NCRS. Used with permission.

NCRS 1963-1967 Chassis
Page 2 of 4 — Revised 11/02

Name _____ VIN _____ Model _____ Year _____

5. Engine Cooling System — Originality: 45 Condition: 35 Total: 80

5	4	Fan
5	4	Fan clutch
15	10	Radiator & mounting
6	6	Shrouds & seals
5	4	Core support
6	5	Expansion tank, mounting, cap, overflow & return hoses/clamps
3	2	Decal(s), label(s) & stamp(s)

6. Front Valance Area — Originality: 22 Condition: 18 Total: 40

7	5	Horns
6	6	Headlight motors & switches
3	3	Valance area braces, wiring & clips
6	4	Valance area fiberglass & blackout

7. Front Suspension — Originality: 35 Condition: 35 Total: 70

5	5	Anti-roll bar, links & bushings
5	5	Lower A arms, ball joints & hardware
10	10	Knuckles, spindles, arms & brake assemblies
4	4	Front springs
5	5	Front shocks & bushings
6	6	Steering linkage, idler, stabilizer or PS slave cylinder (if equipped)

8. Starter System — Originality: 16 Condition: 14 Total: 30

12	10	Starter motor
2	2	Solenoid
2	2	Brace, heat shield & wire guide (if equipped)

9. Oil Pan & Filter — Originality: 14 Condition: 11 Total: 25

| 8 | 7 | Oil pan & drain plug |
| 6 | 6 | Oil filter & instructions |

10. Transmission *(Judge A or B only, Check Box)* — Originality: 25 Condition: 20 Total: 45

A. Standard Transmission 3 / 4 spd ☐

15	10	Transmission
4	4	Bellhousing & inspection cover
6	6	Clutch actuating assembly

For tabulation use only
☐ + ☐ = ☐ Deduction subtotal, page 2 of 4
Tabulator initial ☐ ☐

NCRS 1963–1967 Chassis Scoring Sheets (2 of 4)
Copyright © NCRS. Used with permission.

NCRS 1963-1967 Chassis
Page 3 of 4 — Revised 11/02

Name _____
VIN _____
Model _____ Year _____

		10. Transmission (Judge A or B only, Check Box) (continued)	Originality: 25	Condition: 20	Total: 45
		B. Automatic Transmission ☐			
15	10	Transmission			
3	3	Kickdown linkage assembly			
3	3	Fluid fill, dipstick, & vacuum line			
4	4	Fluid cooler & lines			

		11. Frame	Originality: 30	Condition: 30	Total: 60
15	15	Frame & numbers			
5	5	Body mounting, shims, marks & cushions			
5	5	Parking brake cables & hardware			
5	5	Brake/fuel lines, blocks & clips			

		12. Exhaust System	Originality: 20	Condition: 20	Total: 40
10	10	Exhaust pipes & mufflers			
5	5	Mounting, hangers & clamps			
5	5	Heat shields, ground straps & exhaust tips			

		13. Rear Suspension	Originality: 35	Condition: 35	Total: 70
5	5	Spring assembly, mounting & cushions			
5	5	Differential & yokes			
5	5	Driveshaft & halfshaft assemblies			
5	5	Strut rod assemblies & stabilizer bar assembly (if equipped)			
5	5	Trailing arm assemblies & spindle support			
5	5	Shocks & bushings			
5	5	Brake assemblies			

		14. Underbody & Tank	Originality: 25	Condition: 25	Total: 50
17	17	Underbody fiberglass & attaching reinforcements			
8	8	Fuel tank & mounting			

		15. Overall Cleanliness	Originality: none	Condition: 20	Total: 20
none	20	Overall cleanliness of items 1-14			

For tabulation use only
☐ + ☐ = ☐ Deduction subtotal, page 3 of 4
Tabulator initial ☐ ☐

NCRS 1963–1967 Chassis Scoring Sheets (3 of 4)
Copyright © NCRS. Used with permission.

NCRS 1963-1967 Chassis
Page 4 of 4 — Revised 11/02

Name _____
VIN _____
Model _____ Year _____

Review

Judge _____   Judge _____

Owner review & initial ☐   Team Leader review & initial ☐   Judging Chairman review & initial ☐

For tabulation use only

Page 1 subtotal = ☐
Page 2 subtotal = ☐
Page 3 subtotal = ☐   Tabulator initial ☐ ☐

Total deduction ☐ (Subtract from 700 possible) − 700
Total Chassis ☐

Transfer score to Scoring Summary & Judging Summary Sheets

NCRS 1963–1967 Chassis Scoring Sheets (4 of 4)
Copyright © NCRS. Used with permission.

1963-67 NCRS PERFORMANCE VERIFICATION TEST

Owner: _____ Membership #: _____ Date: _____

Address: _____

City: _____ State: _____ Zip: _____

Location of Meet: _____ ☐ Driven ☐ Trailered

Model Year: _____ VIN: _____ Color: _____ H.P.: _____

Insurance Company: _____ Policy #: _____ Expires: _____

Important: Prior to beginning test, owner must review Judging Reference Manual and 1963-67 Operations Manual & PV Test Guide for test prerequisites and requirements including: Expected component function, seat belt use, engine RPM requirement, single malfunction repair and failure. Conduct test in order listed, circling each pass. Note specific reason for test failure. Conduct test in safe legal manner.

- Verifier is to score by circling "Pass" or "Fail" at right-hand column; one failure terminates test.

PRETEST
Pretest: Owner, Third Flight, Liability Insurance, VIN Plate, Registration, License Plate(s),
 Driver's License, Tire Type, Wheelcovers/caps in place .... Yes No
Pretest: Cold Engine Check .... Yes No
Pretest: Car Conforms to Performance Verification Standard .... Yes No

THE TEST STARTS NOW
Prestart Fuel Leaks .... Pass Fail
Prestart Choke/Fast Idle Engagement .... Pass Fail
Prestart Fan & Fan Clutch Check .... Pass Fail
Prestart Powerglide Starter Neutral Safety Switch (if equipped) .. Pass Fail

START ENGINE
Engine Start, Backfire .... Pass Fail
Starter Motor Cranking & Battery .... Pass Fail
Choke Setting & Operation .... Pass Fail
Fast Idle Function & Engine Speed .... Pass Fail
Exhaust System Leaks & Rattles .... Pass Fail
Initial Fluid Leak Check In Engine Compartment & Under Car ..... Pass Fail
Exhaust Emission, Mufflers & Noise Level .... Pass Fail
Heat Riser Valve Function (if equipped) .... Pass Fail
Automatic Idle Kickdown Function & Normal Idle Engine Speed .... Pass Fail
Engine Noise, Misfire, Vibration, Lifters (correct type), & Crankcase Blow-by .. Pass Fail
Valve Lifters: Type & Appropriate Application .... Pass Fail
Engine Belt(s) Squeal (accelerate engine) .... Pass Fail
Windshield Wipers, Two-Speeds, & Self-Parking .... Pass Fail
Windshield Washers: Function, Switch Activation & Coverage ..... Pass Fail

STOP ENGINE (Wipe Washer Fluid Run-off)
Clock, Type, Reset & Time of Day Notation: _____ Pass Fail
Courtesy Lamps, Door Remote Switches & Headlight Switch Detent .. Pass Fail
Seat Tracks: Release, Movement, Settings & Lock .... Pass Fail
1967 Seat Back Tilt, Latching, Release & Lock .... Pass Fail
Glove Compartment Door Operation & Compartment Lamp .... Pass Fail
Glove Compartment Lock & Key Function .... Pass Fail
Side Window Operation, Sealing & Power Assist (if equipped) .... Pass Fail
Vent Window Operation & Sealing .... Pass Fail
Interior Door Locks & Door Latch Function .... Pass Fail
Cigarette Lighter Function .... Pass Fail

Page 1

1963–67 NCRS Performance Verification
Test Scoring Sheets (1 of 4)
Copyright © NCRS. Used with permission.

1963-67 NCRS PERFORMANCE VERIFICATION TEST

Ash Tray: Cover Function & Removal Ability .... Pass Fail
Ignition Switch & Key Function .... Pass Fail
Interior Rearview Mirror Adjustment & Holding Ability (including Day/Nite, if equipped) .. Pass Fail
Telescopic Steering Column Function (1965-67 only, if equipped) .. Pass Fail
Headrests: Movement & Settings (1966-67 only, if equipped) .... Pass Fail
Hood Latching & Release Function .... Pass Fail
Hood Hinges & Support .... Pass Fail
Horns: Hi/Low Tone, Volume & Horn Button Function (with tele. column "in" & "extended") .. Pass Fail
Exterior Door Latch Mechanism & Function .... Pass Fail
Exterior Door Lock & Key Function (verify key) .... Pass Fail
Door Hinge Operation .... Pass Fail
Exterior Rearview Mirror Adjustment & Holding Ability .... Pass Fail
Convertible Top Compartment Deck Release & Rear Bow Latching Mechanism .. Pass Fail
Soft/Hardtop Header Latches .... Pass Fail
Folding Convertible Top Operation .... Pass Fail
Hardtop Removal & Replacement .... Pass Fail
Luggage Area Exhaust Fan Operation (1964-65 coupes only) ...... Pass Fail
Fuel Filler Door Catch & Hinge .... Pass Fail
Extendable Radio Antenna (1963-64, if radio equipped) .... Pass Fail
Power Antenna Operation (1965-66, all if radio equipped) ...... Pass Fail
Fixed Height Radio Antenna: Verify Type (1967, if radio equipped) .. Pass Fail
Spare Tire Carrier & Lock Function (verify key) .... Pass Fail
Tire Tool Function & Jack Operation .... Pass Fail

RESTART ENGINE
Restart .... Pass Fail
Headlamp Motors: Operation .... Pass Fail
Low Beam Headlamps .... Pass Fail
High Beam Headlamps .... Pass Fail
Front Parking Lamps .... Pass Fail
Front Turn Signals (with parking lamps on) .... Pass Fail
Rear Turn Signals (with parking lamps on) .... Pass Fail
Emergency Hazard Flasher Switch & Lamps (optional 1966; standard 1967) .. Pass Fail
Brake Lights .... Pass Fail
Taillights .... Pass Fail
License Plate Lamp .... Pass Fail
Back-up Lamps (optional 1963-65; standard 1966-67) .... Pass Fail
Fuel Gauge Function .... Pass Fail
Oil Pressure Gauge Function .... Pass Fail
Temperature Gauge Function .... Pass Fail
Ammeter Guage Function .... Pass Fail
Tachometer & Appropriate Redline .... Pass Fail
Radio: Type & Appropriate Application (if equipped) .... Pass Fail
AM Wonderbar Radio: Function, Tone, Volume & Interference ..... Pass Fail
AM/FM Radio: Function, Tone, Volume & Interference .... Pass Fail
Heater & Defroster: Function & Controls .... Pass Fail
Air Conditioning System & Cable Control Operation .... Pass Fail
Air Conditioning Duct Outlet Operation .... Pass Fail

TURN OFF ENGINE

COVER WINDOWS TO FACILITATE INTERIOR LIGHT CHECK
Instrument Panel Gauges: Illumination & Dimming Control .... Pass Fail
Speedometer & Tachometer: Illumination & Dimming Control ...... Pass Fail
Radio (if equipped): Dial Illumination & Dimming Control (w/Key & Radio ON) .. Pass Fail
Clock: Illumination & Dimming Control .... Pass Fail

Page 2

1963–67 NCRS Performance Verification
Test Scoring Sheets (2 of 4)
Copyright © NCRS. Used with permission.

1963-67 NCRS PERFORMANCE VERIFICATION TEST

Cigarette Lighter Well: Illumination & Dimming Control .... Pass Fail
Ignition Switch Key Well: Illumination & Dimming Control .... Pass Fail
Heater/AC Control Identification Bezels: Illumination & Dimming Control .... Pass Fail
Direction Signal Indicators: Illumination & Flash .... Pass Fail
Headlamp Motor Position Alarm: Illumination & Flash .... Pass Fail
Headlamp High Beam Indicator: Illumination .... Pass Fail
Parking Brake Alarm: Illumination & 1963-66 Flash .... Pass Fail

INTERIOR LIGHT CHECK COMPLETE – Uncover Windows
Parking Brake Lever Function .... Pass Fail
Seat Belt Adjustment & Buckle Function .... Pass Fail
Car Stance & Outer Tie Rod End Location .... Pass Fail

RESTART ENGINE & DEPART ON ROAD TEST

TEN-MILE ROAD TEST
Engine Restart .... Pass Fail
Odometer Reading Notation:_____ .... Pass Fail
Trip Odometer Reading Notation:_____ .... Pass Fail
Acceleration to 90% of Redline .... Pass Fail
Deceleration, Backfire .... Pass Fail
Speedometer: Reading, Noise & Needle Bounce .... Pass Fail
Speed Warning Indicator Function (optional, 1967 only) .... Pass Fail
Tachometer: Reading, Noise, & Needle Bounce .... Pass Fail
Fuel, Oil Pressure, Temperature & Ammeter Gauges During Road Test .... Pass Fail
Automatic Right & Left Turn Signal Cancellation Function .... Pass Fail
Lane Change Direction Signal Function (1967 only) .... Pass Fail
Sunshades: Movement & Retention .... Pass Fail
Kick Panel Cowl Vents & Cable Operation .... Pass Fail

MANUAL TRANSMISSION
Type & Appropriate Application .... Pass Fail
Bearing or Excessive Gear Noise .... Pass Fail
Throwout Bearing Noise .... Pass Fail
Gear Engagement & Shifting, Up & Down .... Pass Fail
Shifting Linkage Throw (long throw only) & Noise .... Pass Fail
Gear Retention Under Acceleration .... Pass Fail
Gear Retention Under Deceleration .... Pass Fail
Reverse Gear, Backing & 4-Speed Lockout Function .... Pass Fail
Clutch Chatter or Slippage .... Pass Fail
Manual Transmission Shifter Boot Seal .... Pass Fail

POWERGLIDE AUTOMATIC TRANSMISSION
Type & Application .... Pass Fail
Powerglide Shift Lever/Pattern, 1965-67 Detent Button & Park Function .... Pass Fail
Excessive Noise .... Pass Fail
Gear Engagement .... Pass Fail
Torque Converter Slippage .... Pass Fail
Automatic Gear Shift, Upshift at Correct Shiftpoint .... Pass Fail
Automatic Downshift at Correct Shiftpoint .... Pass Fail
Ability to Shift Manually, Up & Down .... Pass Fail
Throttle Acceleration Kickdown (Passing) Gear .... Pass Fail
Reverse Gear & Backing .... Pass Fail
Park Range & Function .... Pass Fail
Powerglide Transmission Shifter Boot Seal .... Pass Fail

REAR AXLE
Differential Gear, Bearings or Axle Bearing Noise .... Pass Fail

Page 3

1963–67 NCRS Performance Verification
Test Scoring Sheets (3 of 4)
Copyright © NCRS. Used with permission.

1963-67 NCRS PERFORMANCE VERIFICATION TEST

Driveshaft, Universal Joint Noise or Vibration .... Pass Fail
Positraction (if equipped) Chatter/Sticking .... Pass Fail

BRAKES
Brake Squeal, Out-of-Round Drums or Rotor Pulsation .... Pass Fail
Brake Pull to Left or Right With Firm Application .... Pass Fail

STEERING & HANDLING
Indexing of Steering Wheel Center & Horn Button Center .... Pass Fail
Tracking Ability in Straight Line .... Pass Fail
Steering Linkage, Control Arms, Tie Rod End Wear .... Pass Fail
Steering Gear Box Wear, Excessive Freeplay .... Pass Fail
Steering Return .... Pass Fail
Suspension, Excessive Body Roll, Right & Left Turns .... Pass Fail
Suspension, Excessive Body Shift Under Acceleration or Braking .... Pass Fail
Wheel Balance, Hop or Shimmy .... Pass Fail

GENERAL PERFORMANCE
Squeaks & Rattles .... Pass Fail
General Tightness of Vehicle .... Pass Fail
Wind Drafts Due to Improper Side Window or Top Sealing .... Pass Fail

FOLLOWING ROAD TEST
Odometer Accuracy Reading:_____ & Miles Driven Computation:_____ .... Pass Fail
Trip Odometer Accuracy Reading:_____ .... Pass Fail
Parking Brake Ability – On Incline – Nose Down .... Pass Fail
Parking Brake Ability – In Gear .... Pass Fail
Power Steering Ability When Stopped .... Pass Fail

STOP ENGINE
Engine Dieseling or Run-On .... Pass Fail
Fuel Leaks .... Pass Fail
Boil-Over or Coolant Leaks .... Pass Fail
Heater Hose Leaks .... Pass Fail
Engine Oil Leaks .... Pass Fail
Power Steering Pump & Slave Cylinder Oil Leaks .... Pass Fail
Air Conditioning Compressor Leaks .... Pass Fail
Transmission Oil/Fluid Leaks .... Pass Fail
Differential or Pinion Seal Oil Leaks .... Pass Fail
Wheel Brake Cylinder or Caliper Leaks .... Pass Fail
Shock Absorber Leaks .... Pass Fail
Master Brake Cylinder Leaks at Engine Compartment .... Pass Fail
Clutch Pedal (if equipped), Throw, Spring Counterbalance, Freeplay & Return .... Pass Fail
Brake Pedal, Travel, Firmness, Spring Assisted Return .... Pass Fail
Brake Lights Switch Adjustment (check ammeter discharge) .... Pass Fail
Interior Brake Fluid Leak at Master Cylinder .... Pass Fail
Note Time of Day on Clock Since Initial Check & Notation:_____ .... Pass Fail
Interior & Exterior Rearview Mirrors Maintain Position During Test Drive .... Pass Fail
Loose or Falling parts .... Pass Fail
Unusual Occurrences During Test .... Pass Fail
Any Necessary Recheck .... Pass Fail

END OF TEST

Performance Verifier:_____ Test: ☐ PASS ☐ FAIL
4/96   (signature)

Page 4

1963–67 NCRS Performance Verification
Test Scoring Sheets (4 of 4)
Copyright © NCRS. Used with permission.

CHAPTER 6

National Corvette Restorers Society (NCRS) Awards and Events

NCRS Top Flight Award

Of the 20,955 Corvettes that have gone through the NCRS Flight judging, 15,520 have received a Top Flight Award, as of October 27, 2016.

NCRS Performance Verification (PV) Award

Only 1,469 have received a PV Award, as of October 27, 2016.

NCRS Zora Arkus-Duntov Mark of Excellence Award

This award requires attendance at a minimum of three events and must be completed within a three-year period. Only 1,028 Corvettes have achieved the NCRS Zora Arkus-Duntov Mark of Excellence Award, as of October 27, 2016.

Awards received and events attended along the way to the Zora Arkus-Duntov Mark of Excellence Award:

2005-07 NCRS National Convention, Park City, Utah
Zora Arkus-Duntov Mark of Excellence Award

2005-07 NCRS National Convention, Park City, Utah
Top Flight Award—score 97.0

2004-07 NCRS National Convention, Windsor, Ontario, Canada
Performance Verification Test—pass

2004-04 Lowe's Motor Speedway NCRS Regional Meet, Charlotte, North Carolina
Top Flight Award—score 98.0

2003-06 NCRS National Convention, Hershey, Pennsylvania
Performance Verification Test—failed

2003-07 NCRS 7 Springs Regional Meet, 7 Springs, Pennsylvania
Performance Verification Test—failed

2003-04 Stone Mountain Regional Meet, Atlanta, Georgia
Performance Verification Test—failed

2002-09 Garden State NCRS Regional Meet, Woodbridge, New Jersey
Performance Verification Test—failed

2001-05 NCRS Mid-Atlantic Chapter Meet, Front Royal, Virginia
Top Flight Award—score 98.1

2000-10 Delaware Valley Chapter Meet, Jenkintown, Pennsylvania
Top Flight Award—score 98.5

2000-08 Delaware Valley Chapter Meet, Carlisle, Pennsylvania
Top Flight Award—score 98.1

FOR THE RESTORATION AND PRESERVATION OF CORVETTES

Great Cars & Great Friends

July 21, 2005

Congratulations Paul,

It gives us great pleasure to honor you with the highest concours award offered by NCRS, the NCRS-Duntov Mark of Excellence Award. This award is presented to you, the owner, in recognition of the long hours of preparation required to meet the requirements with your Yellow 1966 427 Corvette, Serial Number 194376S115422. This award was developed as the ultimate concours award for a Corvette and is shared by only the few who have been willing to make the sacrifices necessary. Reaching a score above 97 twice, once at a National Convention, is surmounted only by the passing of the Performance Verification Test, which is a real feat both physically and emotionally. You should be proud.

You have received your plaque at the 2005 National Convention in Park City, UT. We encourage you to bring the 1966 back to future conventions for display. Your Corvette, when verified by the National Team Leader, will earn a plate listing the year and location, which can be affixed to the bottom of your plaque.

Again, congratulations on the ultimate Corvette achievement.

Sincerely,

Gilbert Scrivner
NCRS President

Roy Sinor
NCRS Judging Chairman

National Corvette Restorers Society, Zora Arkus-Duntov Mark of Excellence Award letter.
Copyright © NCRS. Used with permission.

TOP FLIGHT AWARD

This Certificate of Achievement is Presented to

Paul Fritz

For Excellence in the Restoration and Preservation of

1966 Corvette Number **194376S115422**

by the

NATIONAL CORVETTE RESTORERS SOCIETY

Meet: 2005 Convention Park City, Utah
No.: 33-46
Date: 2005 July 17-21
Chief Judge: Roy L. Sinor, Park City

Top Flight Award certificate, Park City, Utah, NCRS National Meeting, July 17–21, 2005. Copyright © NCRS. Used with permission.

Zora Arkus-Duntov Mark of Excellence Award presented to Paul Fritz by NCRS
President Vito Cimilluca, Park City, Utah, July 17–21 2005.
Copyright © NCRS. Used with permission.
Copyright © 2005. Photograph by Debra Wood. Used with permission.

Zora Arkus-Duntov Mark of Excellence Award plaque, NCRS judging chair Roy Sinor
presenting at NCRS National Meeting, Park City, Utah, July 17–21, 2005.
Copyright © NCRS. Used with permission.
Copyright © 2005. Photograph by Debra Wood. Used with permission.

Windsor, Ontario, Canada, waiting for NCRS judge to start performance verification (PV).
Copyright © 2004. Photograph by Debra Wood. Used with permission.

Performing interior light checks for the PV.
Copyright © 2004. Photograph by Debra Wood. Used with permission.

Paul and NCRS judge ready for the road test portion of the PV.
Copyright © 2004. Photograph by Debra Wood. Used with permission.

Canadian Royal Mounty says, "You are going to do what on my roads? Maybe I don't want to know." Paul's answer: "Only 5,000 rpm in first gear."
Copyright © 2004. Photograph by Debra Wood. Used with permission.

PV award presented to Paul Fritz by NCRS President Vito Cimilluca, Windsor, Ontario, Canada, July 25–29, 2004.
Copyright © 2004. Photograph by Debra Wood. Used with permission.

PV award presented to Paul Fritz by NCRS judging chair Roy Sinor, Windsor, Ontario, Canada, July 25–29, 2004.
Copyright © 2004. Photograph by Debra Wood. Used with permission.

Performance Verification (PV) Award certificate, Windsor, Ontario, Canada, NCRS National Meeting, July 25–29, 2004
Copyright © 2004 NCRS. Used with permission.

TOP FLIGHT AWARD

This Certificate of Achievement is Presented to

Paul Fritz

For Excellence in the Restoration and Preservation of

1966 Corvette Number **194376S115422**

by the

NATIONAL CORVETTE RESTORERS SOCIETY

Meet: Speedway Regional, Concord, NC
No. 31.266 Date 15-17 April 2004
Chief Judge: Reba Whittington

Top Flight Award certificate, Speedway NCRS Regional Meeting, Concord, North Carolina, April 15–17, 2004. Copyright © 2004 NCRS. Used with permission.

On display at the Delaware Valley Chapter NCRS Gallery XVI, Corvettes at Carlisle, Carlisle, Pennsylvania, August 28, 2016.

On display at the Delaware Valley Chapter NCRS Gallery II, NCRS Regional Meeting, Corvettes at Carlisle, Carlisle, Pennsylvania, August 22–25, 2002.

Dear Paul,

On behalf of the entire Delaware Valley Chapter of NCRS we would like to thank you for sharing your beautiful '66 Corvette and your time to the **NCRS GALLERY II**. Our gratitude also goes out to all the other participants and especially to Chip and Bill Miller and their Carlisle Events staff. They made it possible for our chapter to put on such a fantastic venue. We truly appreciate everyone's participation. We hope you found the weekend to be as an enjoyable experience as we did. The **NCRS GALLERY II** served its purpose in giving the public a better understanding of the National Corvette Restorers Society, its goals and purpose.

Sincerely,

Elaine & Frank
Elaine Raisner and Frank Stech, Jr.
NCRS GALLERY CO-Chairpersons

Letter from Delaware Valley Chapter NCRS Gallery II, NCRS Regional Meeting,
Corvettes at Carlisle, Carlisle, Pennsylvania, August 22–25, 2002
Copyright © 2002 NCRS. Used with permission.

TOP FLIGHT AWARD

CHAPTER

This Certificate of Achievement is Presented to

PAUL FRITZ

For Excellence in the Restoration and Preservation of

__1966__ Corvette Number __194376S115422__

by the

NATIONAL CORVETTE RESTORERS SOCIETY

Meet __Front Royal, VA__

No. _____ Date __19 May, 2001__

Chief Judge __Duane Ravenberg__

Top Flight Award, Mid-Atlantic Chapter NCRS, Front Royal, Virginia, May 19, 2001.
Copyright © 2001 NCRS. Used with permission.

TOP FLIGHT AWARD

This Certificate of Achievement is Presented to

Paul Fritz

For Excellence in the Restoration and Preservation of

1966 Corvette Number **194376S115422**

by the

NATIONAL CORVETTE RESTORERS SOCIETY

Meet: **Jenkintown, PA**
No.: **31870** Date: **10-15-00**
Chief Judge: *Frank Stech*

Top Flight Award, Delaware Valley Chapter NCRS, Jenkintown, Pennsylvania, October 15, 2000. Copyright © 2000 NCRS. Used with permission.

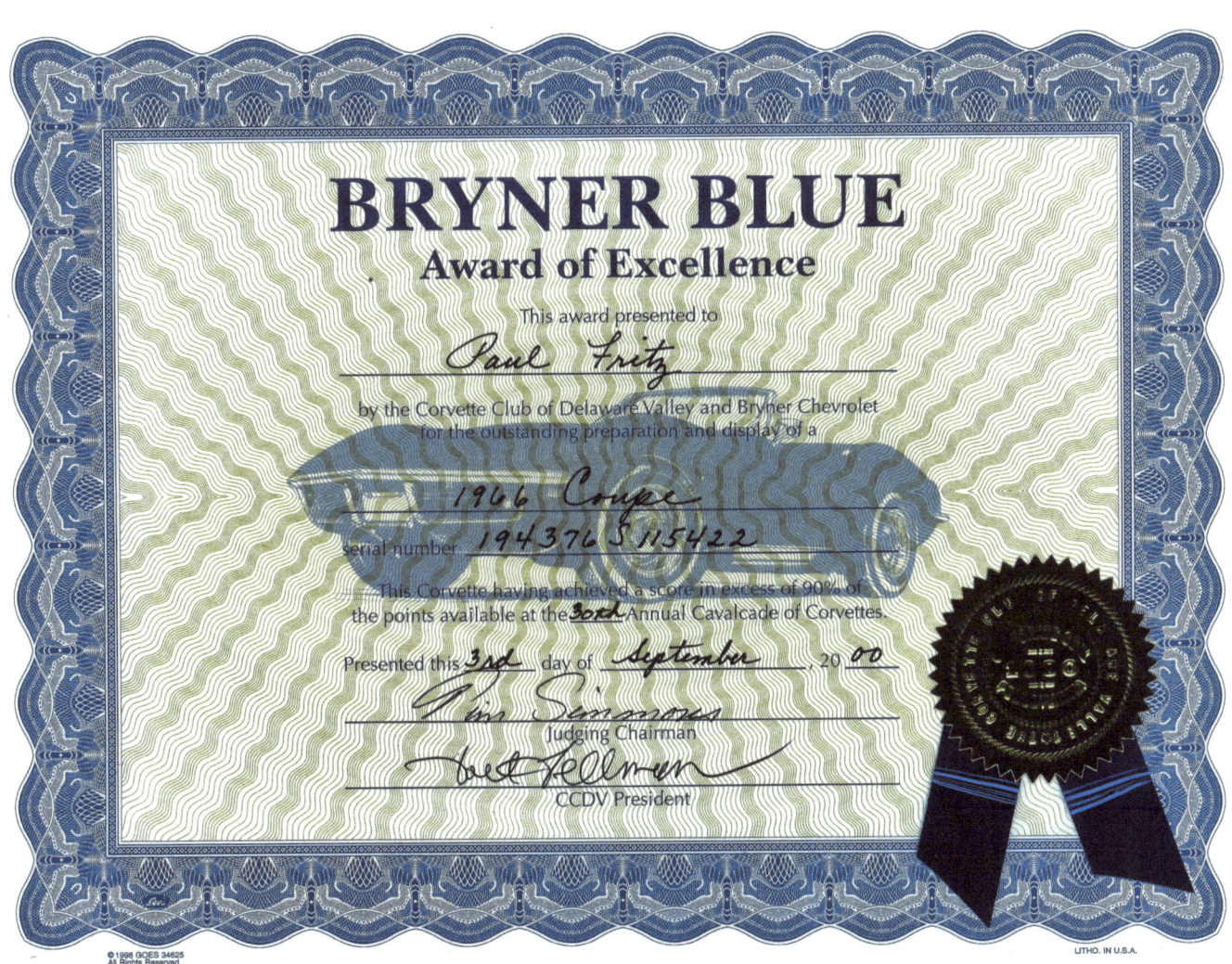

Bryner Blue Award of Excellence, September 3, 2000.
Copyright © 2000 NCRS. Used with permission.

TOP FLIGHT AWARD

This Certificate of Achievement is Presented to

Paul Fritz

For Excellence in the Restoration and Preservation of

1966 Corvette Number **194376S115422**

by the

NATIONAL CORVETTE RESTORERS SOCIETY

Meet **Carlisle, PA**

No. **27-144** Date **8/26/00**

Chief Judge *Frank Stech*

Top Flight Award, NCRS Chapter Delaware Valley, Carlisle, Pennsylvania, August 26, 2000.
Copyright © 2000 NCRS. Used with permission.

The Corvette Restorer

Volume Twenty-Seven
Number Three
Winter 2001

NCRS *Driveline* magazine cover, Carlisle, Pennsylvania, July 2000;
Sunfire Yellow coupe fourth in row, and Paul to right with red shirt.
Copyright © 2000 NCRS. Used with permission.

NCRS *Driveline* magazine cover, Park City, Utah, July 2005. Mine is middle coupe in second row of three Sunfire Yellow coupes by steps at top of page.
Copyright © 2005 NCRS. Used with permission.

NCRS *Driveline* magazine cover, Woodbridge,
New Jersey, September 2001.
Copyright © 2001 NCRS. Used with permission.

NCRS *Driveline* magazine cover, Woodbridge, New
Jersey, September 2001; second row from left,
third from top with all the people around it.
Copyright © 2001 NCRS. Used with permission.

Articles and photos of this 1966 Corvette were in the following publications:

- *Vette Vues* magazine, November 2002
- NCRS Gallery II Participants
- *Carlisle Events* magazine, 2002 Corvettes at Carlisle
- Delaware Valley Chapter NCRS Gallery II Invitational Display
- NCRS Gallery XVI Participants
- *Carlisle Events* magazine, 2016 Corvettes at Carlisle
- Delaware Valley Chapter NCRS Gallery XVI, 2016 Corvettes at Carlisle Invitational Display

CHAPTER 7

Photo Shoot, Rolling Stone/Chevrolet 2004 Calendar–The Year In Rock

A special thank you to Elaine from the Delaware Valley Chapter NCRS for the recommendation to participate in the photo shoot.

The following series of paragraphs is my summary of the e-mails that cover the events that led to the photo shoot for the *Rolling Stone*/Chevrolet 2004 calendar—The Year in Rock.

>   From: NCRS Judging Chairman
>   To;   Paul Fritz
>   Sent: Friday, June 20, 2003 1641
>   Subj: Re: Hershey Meet
>
>   Paul
>
>   We (NCRS) members provide the majority of the Corvettes photographed by Campbell-Ewald for General Motors (GM).
>
>   How close are you to Glen Cove, Long Island? We need to use a silver 63 or yellow 66 for a Rolling Stone Calendar and Magazine; basically the car and a musician will be photographed. There will be a promotion package that the owner gets plus a signed autographed picture and calendar. I'm sure extra prints could be arranged. Your car would need to be there 1 day July 7th. Interested?
>
>   Roy

From: Paul Fritz
To;   NCRS Judging Chairman
Sent: Friday, June 20, 2003 1730
Subj: RE: Hershey Meet

Of course my answer is yes I can do it.

Paul

From: NCRS Judging Chairman
To;   Paul Fritz
Sent: Saturday, June 21, 1043
Subj: Re: Hershey Meet

Paul:

I found a silver 63 coupe the first choice for the calendar shoot. Maybe next time we can get yours. If something falls through on the 63 I will keep you in mind.

Roy

The following is a summary of e-mails between a Campbell-Ewald representative and me.

    From: Campbell-Ewald Representative
    To;   Paul Fritz
    Sent: Monday, June 30, 2003 1059
    Subj: Corvette Images

Paul:

Thanks for your assistance on this request, please forward the images you have to the email address above

Thanks
Campbell-Ewald Representative.

    From: Paul Fritz
    To;   Campbell-Ewald Representative
    Sent: Monday, June 30, 2003 1805
    Subj: Corvette Images

As requested the copies of my 1966 Sunfire Yellow 427/425 Coupe. Best electronic photo's on short notice. Please send more details for planning purposes. Example: date, time, location. My travel time is approximately 300 miles, no problems.

Thanks
Paul

From: Campbell-Ewald Representative
To;   Paul Fritz
CC: Program Manager, Chevrolet Club Connection
Sent: Monday, June 30, 2003 1059
Subj: RE: Corvette Images

Paul:

Thanks for the images of the Corvette, What a beautiful car!

We would love to be able to include your Vette in the upcoming Chevrolet/Rolling Stone Calendar shoot with Ashanti.

As you know the shoot is scheduled for Monday 7/7. It will be a daytime shoot although at this point I am still awaiting the final location and timing from Rolling Stone.

I will pass this info along tomorrow, along with contact names and phone numbers for those attending the shoot. I apologize for not being able to provide today.

Thanks for your participation. I will be in touch. Please do not hesitate to call with any questions.

Campbell-Ewald Representative

From: Campbell-Ewald Representative
To; Paul Fritz
CC: Program Manager, Chevrolet Club Connection
Wenner Media Representative
Sent: Wednesday, July 02, 2003 1516
Subj: Rolling Stone Shoot

Paul:

Still working on the final location for the shoot on Monday. I understand that they are still scouting park locations in and around Glen Cove, Long Island. However, I do know that the shoot is scheduled for the afternoon on Monday 7/7 with Ashanti.

We would like to have you there at approx. 10-11 AM in order to work on lighting etc.

I will not be attending the shoot, so I am providing contact name and phone numbers for the Rolling Stone Representative. He will be your contact upon arrival.

We will follow up to confirm exact location tomorrow am.

Thanks and have fun at the shoot!

Campbell-Ewald Representative

From:	Wenner Media Representative
To;	Paul Fritz
	Campbell-Ewald Representative
CC:	Program Manager, Chevrolet Club Connection
Sent:	Thursday, July 03, 2003 1237
Subj:	Rolling Stone Shoot

Paul:

Looking forward to meeting on Monday. Your car is perfect for the calendar and Ashanti will look fantastic with it. I should have a full call sheet by the end of the day – but here is what I know so far.

We will be meeting in the Morgan Beach parking lot which is at Germaine St and Landing Road.

http/www.glencove-li.com/parkrec.htm

We'd like to have the car there no later than 1100. Ashanti will be getting there around 1330 for hair/makeup and the shoot will take place from 1600-2000.

My office number is X and my cell phone is X if you have any questions.

Thanks

Wenner Media Corporate Marketing Representative
Rolling Stone/US Weekly/Men's Journal

From: Wenner Media Corporate Marketing Representative
        Rolling Stone/US Weekly/Men's Journal
To: Paul Fritz
        Campbell-Ewald Representative
CC: Program Manager, Chevrolet Club Connection
        RSIW Wenner Media
Sent: Thursday, July 03, 2003 1706
Subj: Rolling Stone Shoot

Attached is the all sheet for the shoot on Monday, July 7 with Ashanti - - you will find contact numbers, the location address, schedule, etc.

If you have any questions for further information - - do not hesitate to give me a call over the weekend on my cell phone

Thanks

Wenner Media Corporate Marketing Representative
Rolling Stone/US Weekly/Men's Journal

Rolling Stone/Chevrolet calendar, The Year in Rock, front cover.
Copyright © 2004 Rolling Stone LLC. All Rights Reserved. Used by permission.
Copyright © 2003 Martin Schoeller. Used with permission.

Rolling Stone/Chevrolet calendar, The Year in Rock, front cover.
Copyright © 2004 Rolling Stone LLC. All Rights Reserved. Used by permission.
Copyright © 2003 Martin Schoeller. Used with permission.

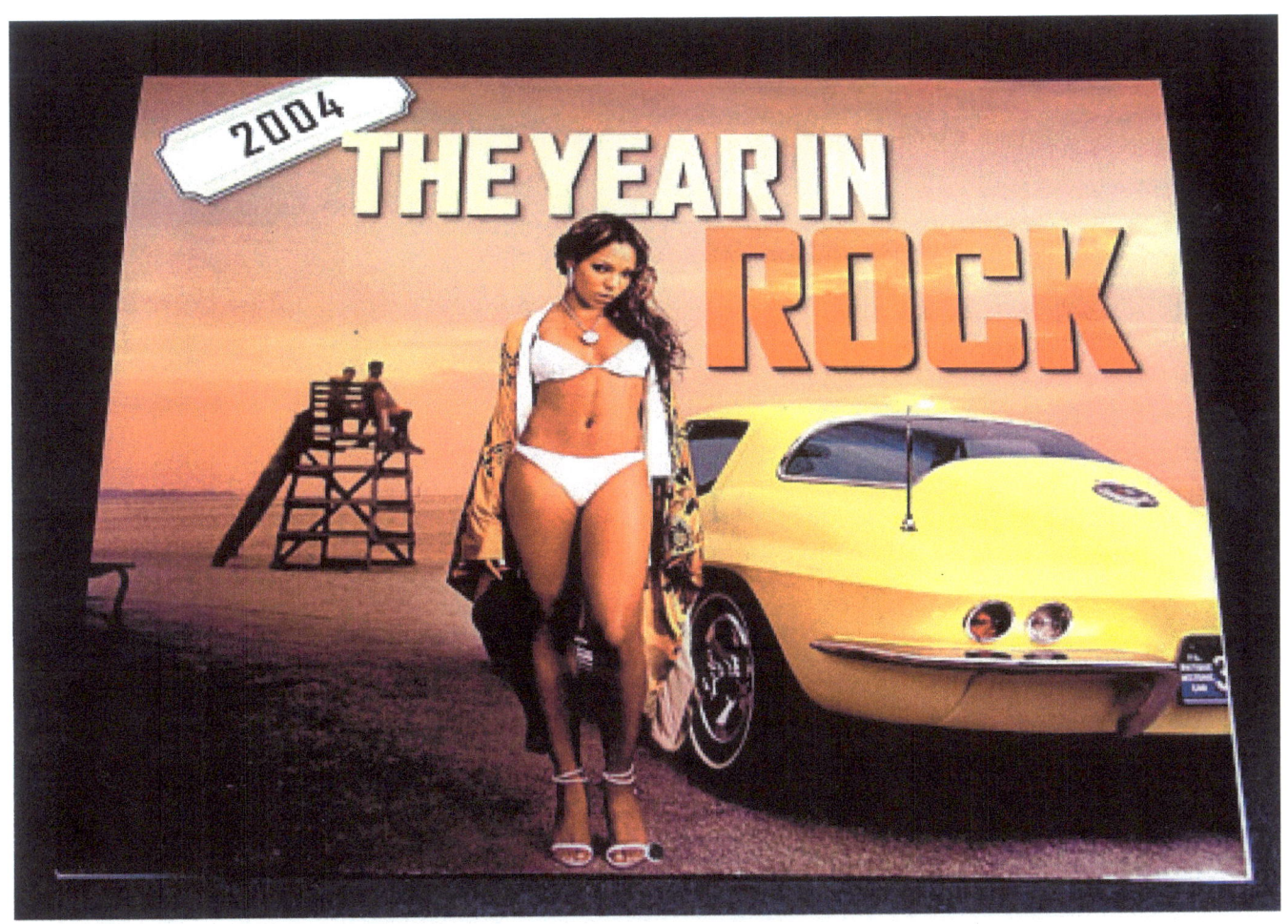

AdAge.com (Jan. 5, 2004) -- The second annual *Rolling Stone* magazine/Chevrolet "Year in Rock" calendar became such a hot advertisement project that rock stars and their labels were clamoring for exposure in it. On the cover, Ashanti steps up to her car promotion duties with sultry gusto.

Rolling Stone/Chevrolet calendar, The Year in Rock, front cover.
Copyright © 2004 Ad Age Crain. Used with permission.
Copyright © 2004 Rolling Stone LLC. All Rights Reserved. Used by permission.
Copyright © 2003 Martin Schoeller. Used with permission.

Rock Stars Clamor to Be in Car Promotion Calendar Chevrolet/ "Rolling Stone" Advertainment Project Is a Hit

By Jean Halliday. Published on January 05, 2004.

DETROIT (AdAge.com) -- In 2002 when General Motors Corp. and Rolling Stone magazine worked to pair music stars and Chevrolet vehicles in photos for a 2003 promotional calendar, they had trouble cajoling recording artists to be part of such an advertainment project.

Rock heavies and their album labels wanted to be in the car promotion calendar. Click to see full image.

But a year later, as the companies put together the 2004 version of the co-branded calendar, it was a very different story in what was becoming a very different music and marketing business.

"We had the record labels calling us trying to get their bands in," said Rolling Stone's publisher, Rob Gregory.

Marketing tool

Mr. Gregory said that in less than a year, the Chevrolet/Rolling Stone "Year in Rock" calendar has become "the best-selling tool I have to show marketers how to capitalize on music and artists in more strategic ways."

Working closely with Chevrolet and its ad agency, Interpublic Group of Cos.' Campbell-Ewald of Warren, Mich., Rolling Stone's Music Consulting Group developed the concept, Mr. Gregory said.

He said 1.5 million calendars were printed for 2004, significantly higher than last year's inaugural run; some will also be available at Chevrolet dealerships and select brand events. Mr. Gregory described Chevrolet as a "major advertiser" in Rolling Stone, which ran 25 advertising pages in 2003. "We tied the calendar to a page commitment from Chevrolet," he said.

Of the $463 million the automaker spent in measured media during the first nine months of 2003, roughly 25%, or $123 million, went into magazines, according to TNS Media Intelligence/CMR.

Music industry upheaval

The first version of the calendar circulated widely during a time when the music distribution industry was grappling with the most dramatic changes in its history and wholeheartedly embracing a concept it has previously largely avoided: the mixing of popular music and advertising into new forms of branded entertainment activities.

The calendar's February stars -- post-grungers Third Eye Blind -- celebrate the car brand's history with a ride in a vintage Impala. Click to see full image.

Observers note that unlike Chrysler Group's glitzy Celine Dion deal, which fared so poorly last year, the calendar project appears to have quietly established a simple but effective advertisement format directly relevant to younger buyers of the fast and fashionable in cars and music.

Mr. Gregory said the first calendar had opened the door to deals with other advertisers, including Coca-Cola Co. and Heineken, and that the concept is now so important to Rolling Stone's ad sales efforts that sales staffers must take the calendar on every call.

"It's [our] best example of the power of the Rolling Stone brand in a co-marketing deal," he said.

The new "Year in Rock" calendar features a bikinied pop star, Ashanti, on the cover next to a 1966 atomic yellow classic Corvette and as Miss July atop a 2004 red Corvette convertible. Melissa Etheridge (January) squints in front of the retro-looking SSR hardtop pickup and Third Eye Blind cruises a drive-in in a vintage Impala convertible (February).

'iconic relationship'

The calendar wants to celebrate that both the cars and the stars have an "iconic relationship," continuing last year's campaign theme that loudly touted the many song lyrics that mention the "Chevy" brand. That campaign was just dropped in favor of the new Chevrolet umbrella theme "An American Revolution" for both its cars and trucks.

Despite the end of the automaker's lyrics campaign, the marketer sees the calendar as a way "to get Chevrolet in front of young customers," a spokesman at Chevrolet said. The brand's connection with popular music and popular culture is still essential, he added.

Chevrolet, which has lost share in the car segment, is readying a slew of crucial vehicle launches it hopes will beef up sales and brand image.

Copyright © 2004 Ad Age Crain. Used with permission.

Ashanti on the beach with 1966 Corvette
J. P. Morgan Park, Glen Cove, Long Island, New York

Ashanti on the beach with 1966 Corvette
J. P. Morgan Park, Glen Cove, Long Island, New York

Ashanti on the beach with 1966 Corvette
J. P. Morgan Park, Glen Cove, Long Island, New York

Paul's Corvette on the beach
J. P. Morgan Park, Glen Cove, Long Island, New York

Highlights of the trip to J. P. Morgan Park, Glen Cove, Long Island, New York

Sunday, July 6, 2003. Departed southern Maryland for J. P. Morgan Park, Glen Cove, Long Island, New York. Along the way, my tow vehicle developed a problem. Driving at 55 mph on Maryland Route 301 north, a few miles from the Delaware line, all the lights on the instrument panel lit up. Only gauge or light that appeared to be working was the tachometer giving a sense of speed. Most troubling was the brake warning light. Now what do I do? Panic set in—and just as quickly common sense. Slow down. Check if brakes work. Slowly pull off the road and come to a stop. That's good. Take a deep breath. Now let's think about troubleshooting. Where to start? If you disconnect the trailer connector, you can check the tow vehicle brakes. With the trailer connector disconnected, place the transmission in drive, ease the pressure on the gas pedal, move forward, and apply the brakes. They work! Now, reconnecting the trailer connector, it must be an electrical problem.

Before continuing my traveling, I will call my buddy in New Jersey and ask his opinion on the problem. After a lengthy discussion, we concluded that it would be safe to continue on and stop at his place to further check out the brake system.

It was late when I arrived at my buddy's place, but we attempted to check out the problem. Not having a lift, it was impossible to get under the vehicle. It was very late, so we decided it was best to get some rest and take the tow vehicle to another buddy's garage in the morning.

Morning of July 7. We put the tow vehicle on the lift at a buddy's garage to troubleshot the mechanical brake system. It checked out good. Next, the electrical system for the brakes. After a few minutes, we found a speed sensor in the left rear wheel to be defective, thereby not giving any speed signal to the computer. Unable to obtain a speed sensor, we decided that it was safe to use the tachometer as a speedometer and continue my trip to New York and the photo shoot.

During the trip, I kept the director of the photo shoot updated with my position and estimated arrival time. Originally I was to have the Corvette at the park at 1000, Monday, July 7, 2003. However, with the problems with the tow vehicle and heavy traffic, I made it to the park at 1400 just in time for the photo shoot.

During the photo shoot, I was taking photos of the setting, the Corvette, and the model they were taking photos of when a six-foot-six security guard approached and said, "No photos." My answer to him was, "Well then I'll take the Corvette home." His reply was, "No problem. I didn't know it was your Corvette." After the photographer was finished shooting, he gave me one of the test photos.

The day was very long, and as I got into northern New Jersey, I pulled into a rest area, crawled into the back of the tow vehicle, and fell asleep for several hours. After waking up, I got a cup of coffee and continued the trip back home to Maryland. After returning home, the tow vehicle was taken to the dealer for servicing.

Both the photo shoot and the travel were great. What an experience!

CHAPTER 8

Photo Shoot, the Danbury Mint Corvette Models

A special thank you to Elaine from the Delaware Valley Chapter NCRS for the recommendation to participate in the photo shoot. This event started when I received a phone call from Elaine, Delaware Valley Chapter NCRS Corvette Club. She asked if I would be interested in having my Corvette photographed for the Danbury Mint to make a model. Yes I was interested in it. She said the photographer would contact me and set up a date and time.

The following e-mails cover the events of the photo shoot for the Danbury Mint Corvette Models.

> From: The Photographer
> Sent: Tuesday, September 30, 2003 3:05 PM
> To: Paul Fritz (fritzpm@olg.com)
> Subject: Photo Shoot
>
> I just spoke with Frank about photographing his 1967 Corvette and would like to try to arrange to shoot your '66 either the day before or the day after. I figure if I can photograph one, get a hotel room close to the second one and do that one the next morning, we'll be all set. That will save me having to travel back and forth from Connecticut each time.
>
> That said, I realize that it might not be possible to do that and if I need to make two separate trips I will. Frank will call me early next week and we'll discuss what works well for him. Let's see if we can lucky with everyone's availability and the weather.
>
> Thanks
> The Photographer

From: Paul Fritz (fritzpm@olg.com)
Sent: Tuesday, September 30, 2003 7:51 PM
To: The Photographer
Subject: RE: Photo Shoot

The Photographer:

My schedule is flexible.
I'll work with you to save trips.
I am about 4 hours south of Phila, PA in southern Maryland.
Will send directions for you.
Look forward to meeting you.

Thanks
Paul

301-737-0444 home
301-904-6152 cell
301-342-5586 work

20622 Davidway
Lexington Park, MD 20653

From: The Photographer
Sent: Wednesday, October 01, 2003 9:07 AM
To: Paul Fritz (fritzpm@olg.com)
Subject: RE: Photo Shoot

I'm always happy to hear that someone's schedule is flexible. It's makes my life MUCH easier.

I guess we'll just have to wait for the call from Frank next week to set everything up.

The best days for me would be either Tuesday and Wednesday or Wednesday and Thursday. My son has a football game Friday night and I never miss those.

I look forward to meeting you as well. Elaine e-mailed me a few pics and the car looks beautiful. (Can't wait to meet the car also)

I'll talk to you as soon as I hear from Frank and figure out a schedule. Pray for good weather.

Thanks for your help,
The Photographer

Photo shoot, my driveway.
Photograph by the Danbury Mint photographer.
Copyright © 2003 MBI/Danbury Mint. Used with permission.

Photo shoot in my driveway.
Photograph by the Danbury Mint photographer.
Copyright © 2003 MBI/Danbury Mint. Used with permission.

Photo shoot, my driveway.
Photograph by the Danbury Mint photographer.
Copyright © 2003 MBI/Danbury Mint. Used with permission.

Photo shoot, my driveway.
Photograph by the Danbury Mint photographer.
Copyright © 2003 MBI/Danbury Mint. Used with permission.

Photo shoot, my driveway.
Photograph by the Danbury Mint photographer.
Copyright © 2003 MBI/Danbury Mint. Used with permission.

Model made from the information gathered from the photo shoot.

CHAPTER 9

Other Awards

It has been a lot of fun showing the Corvette. Here are other forms of recognition received at various shows/events:

- Atlantic City, New Jersey, Convention Center Show and Auction, February 28, 2000.
- Tri-State Corvette Show, Corvettes at Peddlers Village, Concourse 53–67 Award, First Place, October 2000, Peddlers Village, Pennsylvania.
- Tri-State Corvette Show, Corvettes at Peddlers Village, Participation Award, October 2000, Peddlers Village, Pennsylvania.
- Skyline Drive Corvettes Twenty-Second Annual Twilight In-Vette Tational VF Outlet, July 14, 2001, sponsored by Stout Associates Realtors, Reading, Pennsylvania.
- Skyline Drive Corvettes Twenty-Third Annual Twilight In-Vette Tational VF Outlet, July 13, 2002, first place for 63–67 class, Reading, Pennsylvania.
- Southern Maryland Corvette Club, All Corvette Show, Fiftieth Anniversary Participates Choice Best Club Corvette Trophy, courtesy of Little Silences' Rest Inc., St. Mary's Rod and Classic Spring Fling XIV 2004, Leonardtown, Maryland.
- Southern Maryland Corvette Club, All Corvette Show, Sponsors Choice, Callaway A&W 2004, Callaway, Maryland.
- Greater Pottsville Cruise, August 10, 2013, Trophy 1 of 5 in class, Pottsville, Pennsylvania.
- Pottsville Cruise, August 9, 2014, Pottsville, Pennsylvania.
- Schuylkill Valley Corvette Club Show, September 19, 2014, Schuylkill Haven, Pennsylvania.

CHAPTER 10

Special Memories over the Years

On liberty/leave from Aviation Electronics Technician School in Memphis, Tennessee on Memorial Day in 1970, I spent time with my girlfriend. Highlights of the weekend were getting to spend time with my girlfriend and driving the Corvette after five months of school.

Paul and Shelby, Schuylkill Haven, Pennsylvania, May 30, 1970.
Copyright © 1970. Photograph by Eileen. Used with permission.

Now turn the clock to the present. Here we are now in 2005 with sister and friend with the same Corvette in Leonardtown, Maryland, after a show. We all have remained friends over the years. Enjoyable times.

Eileen, Shelby, Paul, Leonardtown, Maryland, August 13, 2005.
Copyright © 2005. Photograph by a friend. Used with permission.

Previous Owners Gathering

Using the bill of sales, shown in chapter 2, "History of Ownership," I was able to track down two of the previous owners. We all got together at the Skyline Drive Corvette Twenty-Second Annual Twilight In-Vette Tational in Reading, Pennsylvania, on July 14, 2001. They kept saying, "She never looked this good when we had it." Interesting note: Harold left his daughter's wedding to come see the Corvette.

Several years later at the Pottsville Cruise in Pottsville, Pennsylvania, on August 9, 2014, I again met up with Warren and had a great reunion with lots of stories. Both of us agreed we did not know what we had when we had it back in late 1969. He wishes he still had this Corvette. He says the new ones are not the same. Agree!

Owner Paul Fritz and previous owners Warren and Harold, Skyline Drive Corvette Twenty-Second Annual Twilight In-Vette Tational, Reading, Pennsylvania, July 14, 2001.
Copyright © 2001. Photograph by Eileen. Used with permission.

Warren, previous owner, at the Pottsville Cruise in Pottsville, Pennsylvania, August 9, 2014.

Dave during the restoration, November 13, 1998–March 3, 2000.

Dave is responsible for the attention to detail during the restoration. As we progressed through the restoration, he learned that I could do good work. We spent many hours together working on the details. His favorite answers to my questions were: "Look it up in the book," or, "What does the book say?"

Tom going through his NCRS judging, 2013.

Tom going through his NCRS judging, 2013.

When Tom decided to have his green Corvette go through the NCRS judging process, we spent several weekends going over the judging process described in chapter 5. When the time came for the first event, we trailered his Corvette to the location for the judging. For the second judging event, I loaned him my trailer. On the way home, the trailer blew a tire. Not his fault. Then on the third trip, he borrowed Zack's trailer and blew a tire on that trip.

Zach with his 1970 Corvette convertible and his NCRS Zora Arkus-Duntov Mark of Excellence Award.

Zach assisting Paul with his performance verification (PV) judging, July 2004.
Copyright © 2004. Photograph by Debra Wood. Used with permission.

Zach and I started our friendship at the Atlantic City event in February 2000. Then in August 2000, we shared judging troubles in Carlisle, Pennsylvania. From that point on, we provided support, encouragement, and expertise in repairing and maintaining high-quality Corvettes and special projects around the garage. Thanks, buddy.

Debra hiding behind the truck and waving at Mount Rushmore.

Debra at Niagara Falls on the Canadian side, a stop on return trip from passing PV.

A special travel partner and photographer who kept me company on some very long trips to obtain the NCRS awards. We had some good times. Thank you.

Stone Mountain, Georgia
Copyright © 2003. Photograph by Debra Wood. Used with permission.

Schuylkill Valley Corvette Club, Best of Show, Schuylkill Haven, Pennsylvania, September 21, 2014.

This was a very special event in many ways. Selection for the Best of Show was done by the owners of the other cars in the show. What an honor. The show was in the park behind Mom's house, which brought back many memories. Warren is a member of the Schuylkill Valley Corvette Club, and we got to visit again. It was a great time.

APPENDIX F

Websites with My 1966 Corvette

The Vette Shop restoration, November 13, 1998–March 3, 2000.
http://www.Corvetterestorationpa.com/RestorationProjects/1966YellowCoupe.htm

"Rock Stars Clamor to Be in Car Promotion Calendar, Chevrolet/"Rolling Stone" Advertainment Project Is a Hit," by Jean Halliday, published January 05, 2004.
http://adage.com/article/news/chevy-rolling-stone-calendar-a-hit-rock-stars/39105/

Photo of Ashanti on beach at J. P. Morgan Park, Glen Cove, Long Island, New York with 1966 Corvette, July 7, 2003.
http://wallpaperose.com/ashanti-in-a-white-bikini-with-a-1966-Corvette-c2-sting-ray-coupe.html

APPENDIX B

New Addition to Paul's Garage

After riding in my buddy Zach's 2006 Corvette black convertible, I got the idea it would be nice to have a newer Corvette. Having a newer Corvette would make it easy to just jump in and drive without all the maintenance, as with the older Corvettes.

One day while driving to a local parts store in June 2010, I spotted this 2006 Monterey Red Corvette convertible on a used car lot. On my way home, I stopped to look at this Corvette, but the sales office was closed. After several trip to look at this Corvette, I stopped to talk with the salesman. We took this Corvette out for a test drive and discussed a price.

Little did he know I had a preapproved check from Navy Federal Credit Union, which was in the amount of the negotiated price.

The 2006 Monterey Red Corvette convertible was a new addition to Paul's garage.

It is a real pleasure to drive, especially with the top down.

2006 Monterey Red Corvette convertible

2006 Monterey Red Corvette convertible

New Addition to Paul's Garage
2006 Monterey Red, Corvette Convertible
1G1YY36UX65119041

RPO #	DESCRIPTION	QTY	RETAILS
1YY67	Base Corvette Convertible	11,151	$52,335.00
3LT	Preferred Equipment Group-Convertible	9,972	3,395.00
CM7	Power Convertible Top (3LT req'd)	8,537	1,995.00
F55	Magnetic Selective Ride Control	5,709	1,695.00
QX3	Chrome Aluminum Wheels	2,803	1,995.00
UE1	OnStar System (3LT req'd)	12,869	695.00
U3U	AM/FM CD DVD Nav XM	17,474	1,600.00
8OU	Monterey Red exterior paint	2,173	750.00
193	Interior color Ebony		
LS2	364 cu. in., 6.0 L SFI 400 hp		
	Manual 6 Speed Transmission		
	Total		$64,460.00

Production Date: 20 February 2006

2006 Production numbers

Coupe	6,598	
Convertible	11,151	
Z06	6,272	
Total	34,023	

Purchase Date: 11 June 2010 by Paul M. Fritz

Copyright © 2015 Michael Bruce Associates, Inc. Used with permission.

APPENDIX C

Cool Corvette Adventures in the Fast Lane

I've had awesome and terrifying experiences with fellow Corvette members at National Corvette Restorers Society (NCRS) meets held at Charlotte Motor Speedway (Lowes) in Charlotte, North Carolina.

Several years ago, in April 2004, a group of NCRS friends gathered to have breakfast together in a Charlotte, North Carolina, hotel before the NCRS judging events started. Someone spoke up and asked the question all of us wanted to ask but were a little too scared to bring up. "So, what is the Richard Petty Ride-Along Experience event on today's itinerary all about?"

One of the local NCRS club members smiled and said, "If you guys are brave enough, you are going for qualifying laps in a NASCAR racecar around Charlotte Motor Speedway (Lowes)."

Suddenly the second round of breakfast I had just deposited on my plate didn't seem like a good idea. Commence butterflies, aggressive toe tapping, and body shaking. Things were starting to get really scary.

As we drove through the track entrance tunnel and made our way into the infield, we saw NASCAR racecars traveling at a high rate of speed through turn 1 and along the bank that leads to turn 2. We could only really see the roof of the cars because the banking is banked at more than three stories high.

Oh, and the noises and smells that the racecars were making sounded and smelled like lots of horsepower. Now, talk about insanely sweaty hands. There were a lot of "oh mans" and some other words that can't be typed here as we made our way to the Petty Ride-Along Experience registration office in the center of the infield.

I instantly thought that I was in the wrong place and should quickly go back to the hotel. Admission: I seriously get nervous driving down steep hills, up high mountains, and on high, narrow bridges that have slight turns (hold the comments, please). I sure as heck wasn't ready for high banks and 170-mph-plus speeds, much less letting someone else drive the racecar. What—am I crazy? My friend Zach and I both agreed we were crazy as we continued to head to the Petty Ride-Along Experience office to sign up for the qualifying laps ride in a NASCAR racecar.

There was no backing out now. However, sometimes in life you have to step out of your comfort zone and try something new, something dangerous. Well, it doesn't get more dangerous than racing cars at Charlotte Motor Speedway (Lowes).

As our group arrived at the Petty Ride-Along Experience office, we were given racing suits and helmets to wear. Then we were handed three pages of waivers to sign. We had to initial a lot of things that seemed important, but to be honest, I really wasn't paying attention to what I was signing. I knew it probably wasn't anything good. My nerves were already through the roof. I didn't need to see words like "serious," "injury," and "death."

Now more of the toe tapping and body shaking started, with more second thoughts about that second helping of breakfast. The sounds of the racecars flying around the track weren't helping matters either.

We started our adventure with the ride-along, meaning we got to sit in the passenger seat while a professional driver who does this all day for a living drove us for what would be NASCAR race qualifying laps.

About six one and 220 pounds, it's a little tough for me to fit through the window opening in a NASCAR racecar. Somebody helped shove me in through the window and then quickly tightened what seemed like hundreds of belts (it really was only five belts, but I was wishing for more) around my waist and chest. Then they attached the head and neck restraint straps from the helmet. I couldn't breathe or move a muscle. I couldn't turn my head. My heart was beating really fast. I tried to look confident. But I was terrified. Like, really scared!

Someone said, "Look this way," as they snapped a photo. The driver probably said something nice to me like, "Good morning. My name is Jimmy," but I wasn't listening. I was too busy giving a death stare to the pit road and track in front of me while trying not to pee my pants. And just like that, we were off, heading down pit road at a speed that felt faster than anything I'd ever gone in real life.

As we merged onto the track, I tried, out of instinct, to look behind me to see if any other cars were coming our way. I forgot, however, that it was impossible for me to turn my head at all. So we continued to merge and hope for the best. Nobody ran into us, so things were good, but turn 1 was approaching, and that banking I saw upon arriving at Charlotte infield was awaiting my arrival. As I looked up, turn 1 wall was rapidly approaching, and it appeared that we were headed straight for the wall. Then, as the confident, skilled driver adjusted the steering wheel to the left, the car settled into a beautiful left turn along the left side of the track. However, we were rapidly approaching the racecar that left the pits just prior to our departure. My buddy Zach was in the lead car, and I was in the second car of a pack of three. *Look out, Zach! Here we come! Move over! Get out of the way!* were my thoughts. Thankfully, we never caught them.

We proceeded to whiz around turn 1 and head along the banking toward turn 2. My body felt like I was going down a roller coaster. My stomach felt weird, and my head felt weirder. That second helping of breakfast was close to getting a second shot at life. Well, I survived as we flew through turn 2 and headed down the backstretch. Life was good. Now as we approach turns 3 and 4, things began to settle down just a little. The signs and fence post were just a blur. When you're going that fast, it actually feels like you're going that fast, if it makes sense. The noises, smells, and shaking of the car never let up. It's like you're holding on for dear life, not in control of anything, for better or worse.

We zipped through the first lap, and as we made our first pass across the start/finish line, the speed increased. I remember thinking something like, *(Blanked, blank, blank), I'm actually doing this!*

The second lap was even faster than the first. We were almost up against the wall, diving into turn 1 again, whizzing through turn 2, down the back stretch, into turns 3 and 4, heading for the start/finish line where the flagman showed us the checkered flag. The deceleration wants to throw you forward in the seat. Thank goodness for all the belts to hold you in the seat. I later learned how fast we were going on each lap. The second lap was our best and fastest, as we topped out at 170 mph.

Charlotte Motor Speedway (Lowes) is 1.5 miles long, but at those speeds, it feels like it's about only a football field in length. As we slowly made our way back to pit road, I couldn't stop thinking about how those NASCAR drivers are insane in amazing ways doing this for over four hundred laps at over 200 mph in thirty-six-plus races a year. That's intense.

My driver and I shook hands, and I unbuckled and slowly wiggled out of the car. I was alive. And it was easily one of the coolest things I've ever done in my life. However, it probably took me around thirty minutes to stop shaking.

That same afternoon, shortly after completing the Petty Ride-Along Experience, we had another experience.

We got the opportunity to drive laps in our own Corvettes around Charlotte Motor Speedway (Lowes). Now was the real test of nerves, driving my 1966 Corvette 427-cubic-inch, 425-horsepower coupe with bias ply tires on the super speedway.

However, we were briefed that this time we were restricted to following the pace-truck at no more than 70 mph, with no passing the Corvettes in front of us. "Stay in line, single file, no passing. Obey the flagman. Follow the pace-truck. Any wild moves deemed unsafe will get you a black flag," meaning you need to immediately return to the pits, if not sooner.

We were all parked in the NASCAR garages for the NCRS judging event. Now it was the mass move from the garage area to pit row for staging by year groups C-1, C-2, C-3, C-4, C-5, and C-6. Parked in front of me was a 1965 convertible owned by a friend of mine, TJ. Later that day, we found out he had a universal joint in one of his half shafts going bad, which would restrict his speed on the track.

Without warning, the pace-truck took off down pit row and on to the track at 70 mph. The cars in front of me followed. Here we go—first gear and then second. I was thinking, *Got to feed more gas, hit third and fourth gear before you get left behind. Oh my gosh!* Suddenly we were down pit row and out on the track. Now it was our time to tame the speedway at Charlotte.

As we merged onto the track, out of instinct I tried to look behind me to see if any other cars were coming. I forgot it was impossible to turn my head and keep a clear view on the track in front of me. So I merged and hoped for the best. Nobody ran into me, so life was good. However, turn 1 was fast approaching, and that banking I saw earlier was fast awaiting my arrival. I continued hitting the gas pedal as hard as I could to maintain the 70 mph pace. As I started through turn 1, the car was responding as I was told it would; it wanted to go to the right up toward the outside wall. So I tightened my grip on the steering wheel and turned left to bring her down close to the infield line. There was no messing around at this point. This was all about survival. Well, to my surprise, I survived turn 1 and flew through turn 2 and headed down the backstretch. Life was good!

Now we were fast approaching turn 3, which was worse than turns 1 and 2. Panic set in. What is the correct position on the track to make it through turns 3 and 4 smoothly? Guess my positioning was not totally correct or I lost some trust because I lost a lot of speed coming out of turn 4 to head down the front stretch. As I started to zip past the start/finish line on the first of four laps, I looked up at the flagman; he was signaling me to pick up speed and close in on the car in front of me. Harder on the gas pedal, I picked up speed. Back through turns 1 and 2, down the back stretch into turns 3 and 4. I was fast approaching the start/finish line and fast closing in on TJ, who was slowing due to a u-joint going bad. TJ started running down along the inside line of the track. So I drift up toward the outside wall of turn 1 to reduce my speed so as to not pass him and get black flagged. Then I remember thinking something like, *(Bad word) (bad word) (bad word), I'm actually doing this. What—am I crazy? What a risk!* (No comments.)

Looking back at the runs down the front stretch, you could see the crowd on pit road cheering at the roar of the 427 in my Sunfire Yellow Corvette as I cruised around the speedway.

However, you never really get comfortable because you keep thinking one bad move can lead to disaster … and you want to avoid disaster.

At the end of the cool-down lap, coming out of turn 4, entering pit road a little too hot, I jammed on the brakes to slow down. I was very thankful that all four wheels had disk brakes.

I made it. It was one of the coolest things I've ever done in my life.

What a thrill.

And it gets even better.

As mentioned, several years later in June 2010, I purchased a 2006 Monterey Red Corvette convertible, LS-2, six-speed manual transmission just in time for the NCRS Charlotte meeting in July. I got to repeat the same adventure with the 2006 Corvette, just as I did with the 1966 Corvette 427 cubic-inch, 425-horsepower, four-speed manual transmission, only this time it was a little different.

The first set of qualifying laps, I did by myself, hitting a top speed of 100 mph. What a thrill. It was completely different from the laps with the 1966. The car was relatively quiet; very little engine noise, and shakes, rattles, and rolls were at a minimum. The car stuck to the track a lot better than the old bias ply tires because of the wide, soft radial tires. It was very easy to control. The faster speed left me with shakes and a queasy stomach when I returned to the pits. Remember, I only owned the 2006 Corvette for less than thirty days. What was I thinking?

After entering the garage area, I loaned my 2006 Corvette to by buddy Zach so he could give his girlfriend, Diane, a thrill and experience driving on the track with a C6 similar to his black 2006 Corvette that was back home. Zach's previous experience on the track was in his 1967 convertible, 350 cubic-inch, Sunfire Yellow Corvette the same time that I drove my 1966 Corvette on the track several years earlier. When Zach returned to the pits, he said, "That was cool." Diane was happy and very excited. She wanted to do it again.

Now it was my turn again to do a second set of qualifying laps. This time I took my friend Tom. Things were going well sitting on pit road. We laughed and joked about what it was like to be on the racetrack. When the pace-truck started down pit road, I accelerated through all six gears before leaving pit road.

As we approached turn 1, Tom looked over at the speedometer and saw as we approached 100 mph. Looking back over at Tom, he appeared to be a little scared as he grabbed hold of the passenger's side door handle and hung on for dear life until we completed the two qualifying laps and entered the pits. Not a word from Tom while on the track. Upon returning to the garage area, Tom finally spoke. He said he would be happy to replace the door handle if he broke it from hanging on. We still laugh about our experiences.

Again, these experiences are some of the coolest things I've ever done in my life. However risky they appear to be, we completed them very safely.

Thank you NCRS, Charlotte Motor Speedway (Lowes), the Petty Ride-Along Experience, and my friends for the one of the greatest experiences in my life.

Appendix D

Photographers

Eileen Gagliardi
Debra (Debbie) Wood
The Vette Shop (Dave Tidwell and Sean Farrell)
Paul Martin Fritz
Martin Schoeller
Ron Dill
Richard L. Schreiter

REFERENCES

Amgwert, John. *NCRS 1953–1967 Corvette Specifications Guide,* volume one, second edition. Illustrations by Tom Anjiras and Dana Forrester. National Corvette Restorers Society, 1998.

Amgwert, John. *NCRS 1953–1967 Corvette Specifications Guide,* fourth edition. Illustrations by Tom Anjiras and Dana Forrester. National Corvette Restorers Society, 1998.

National Corvette Restorers Society. www.NCRS.org.

National Corvette Restorers Society (NCRS). *1966 Fifth Edition Corvette Technical Information Manual and Judging Guide.* Copyright © 2010 NCRS National Corvette Restorers Society (NCRS).

National Corvette Restorers Society (NCRS). *1963–1967 Corvette Operations Manual & Performance Verification Test Guide.* Copyright © 2000 NCRS National Corvette Restorers Society (NCRS).

National Corvette Restorers Society (NCRS). *1953–1996 Eighth Edition Corvette Judging Reference Manual.* Copyright © 2010 NCRS National Corvette Restorers Society (NCRS).

The Corvette Black Book, 1953–2015. Michael Bruce Associates, Inc., 2013. Michael Antonick, president, Post Office Box 1966, Gambier, Ohio 43022. www.Corvetteblackbook.com.

The Danbury Mint. 47 Richards Avenue, Norwalk, CT 06857. Copyright © 2003 MBI/Danbury Mint.

www.ingramcontent.com/pod-product-compliance
Lightning Source LLC
Chambersburg PA
CBHW040911020526
44116CB00026B/29